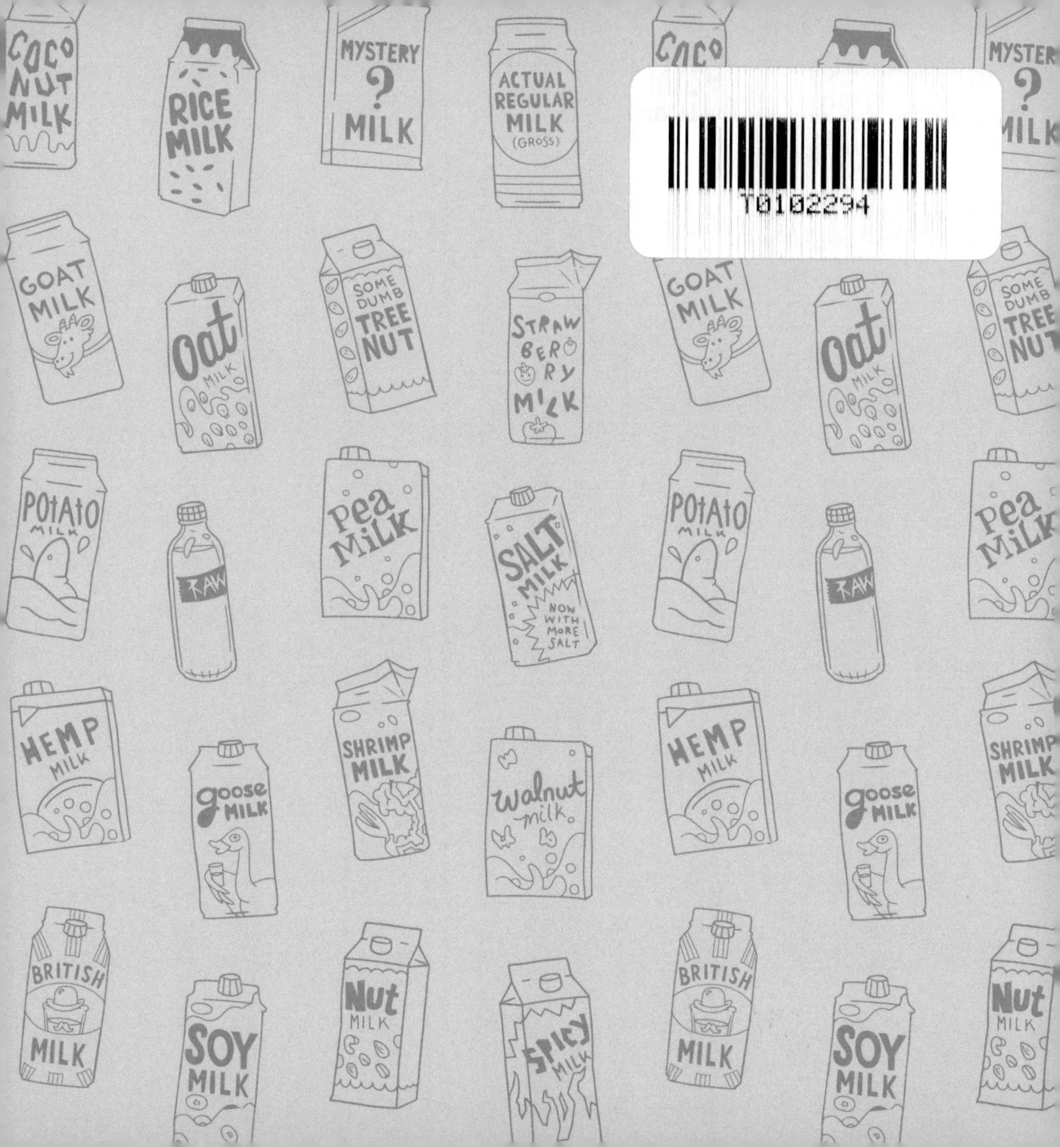
COCO NUT MILK
RICE MILK
MYSTERY ? MILK
ACTUAL REGULAR MILK (GROSS)
COCO
MYSTERY ? MILK
GOAT MILK
Oat MILK
SOME DUMB TREE NUT
STRAWBERRY MILK
GOAT MILK
Oat MILK
SOME DUMB TREE NUT
POTATO MILK
RAW
Pea Milk
SALT MILK NOW WITH MORE SALT
POTATO MILK
RAW
Pea Milk
HEMP MILK
goose MILK
SHRIMP MILK
walnut milk
HEMP MILK
goose MILK
SHRIMP MILK
BRITISH MILK
SOY MILK
Nut MILK
SPICY MILK
BRITISH MILK
SOY MILK
Nut MILK

THERE ARE TOO MANY MILKS

This book covers the hard things about life right now.

If you want to read about old stuff that was hard,
get a history book.

Library of Congress Cataloging-in-Publication Data
Names: Lawall, Tara, author. | Wonder, Anne Marie, author, illustrator.
Title: There are too many milks : and other common annoyances of modern life / by Tara Lawall and Anne Marie Wonder.
Description: San Francisco : Chronicle Books, [2023]
Identifiers: LCCN 2022025632 | ISBN 9781797219875 (hardcover)
Subjects: LCSH: Life--Humor. | Adulthood--Humor. | Conduct of life--Humor. | Capitalism--Social aspects--Humor. | LCGFT: Humor.
Classification: LCC PN6231.L48 L39 2023 | DDC 818/.602--dc23/eng/20220629
LC record available at https://lccn.loc.gov/2022025632.

Manufactured in China.

FSC
www.fsc.org
MIX
Paper | Supporting responsible forestry
FSC™ C008047

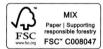

Design by Jon Glick.

10 9 8 7 6 5 4 3 2 1

Chronicle Books LLC
680 Second Street
San Francisco, CA 94107
www.chroniclebooks.com

THERE ARE TOO MANY MILKS

AND OTHER COMMON ANNOYANCES OF MODERN LIFE

By **Tara Lawall** and **Anne Marie Wonder**

CHRONICLE BOOKS

SAN FRANCISCO

It's hard to be a human these days.

BUT I'M A HUMAN.

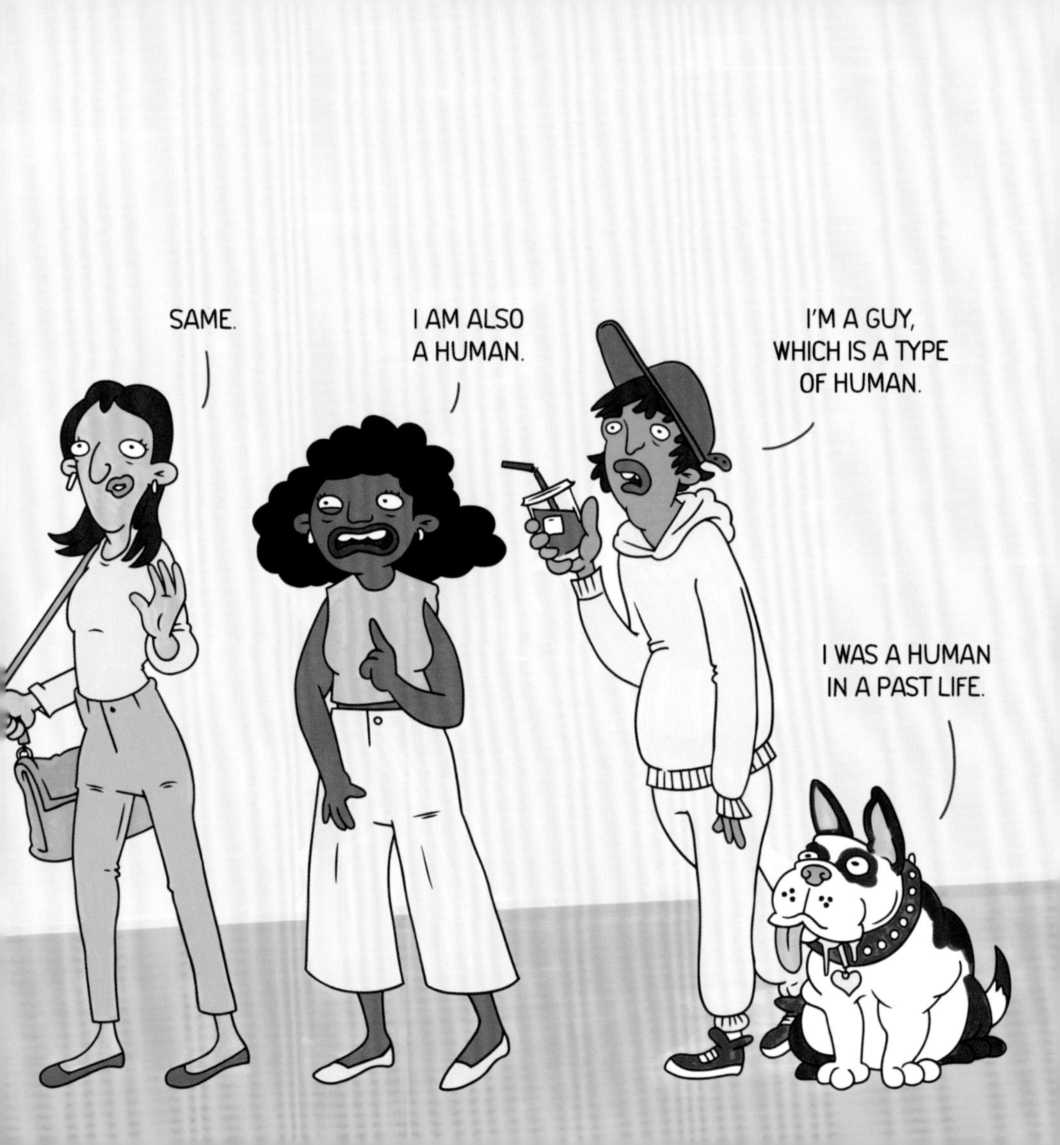
SAME.
I AM ALSO A HUMAN.
I'M A GUY, WHICH IS A TYPE OF HUMAN.
I WAS A HUMAN IN A PAST LIFE.

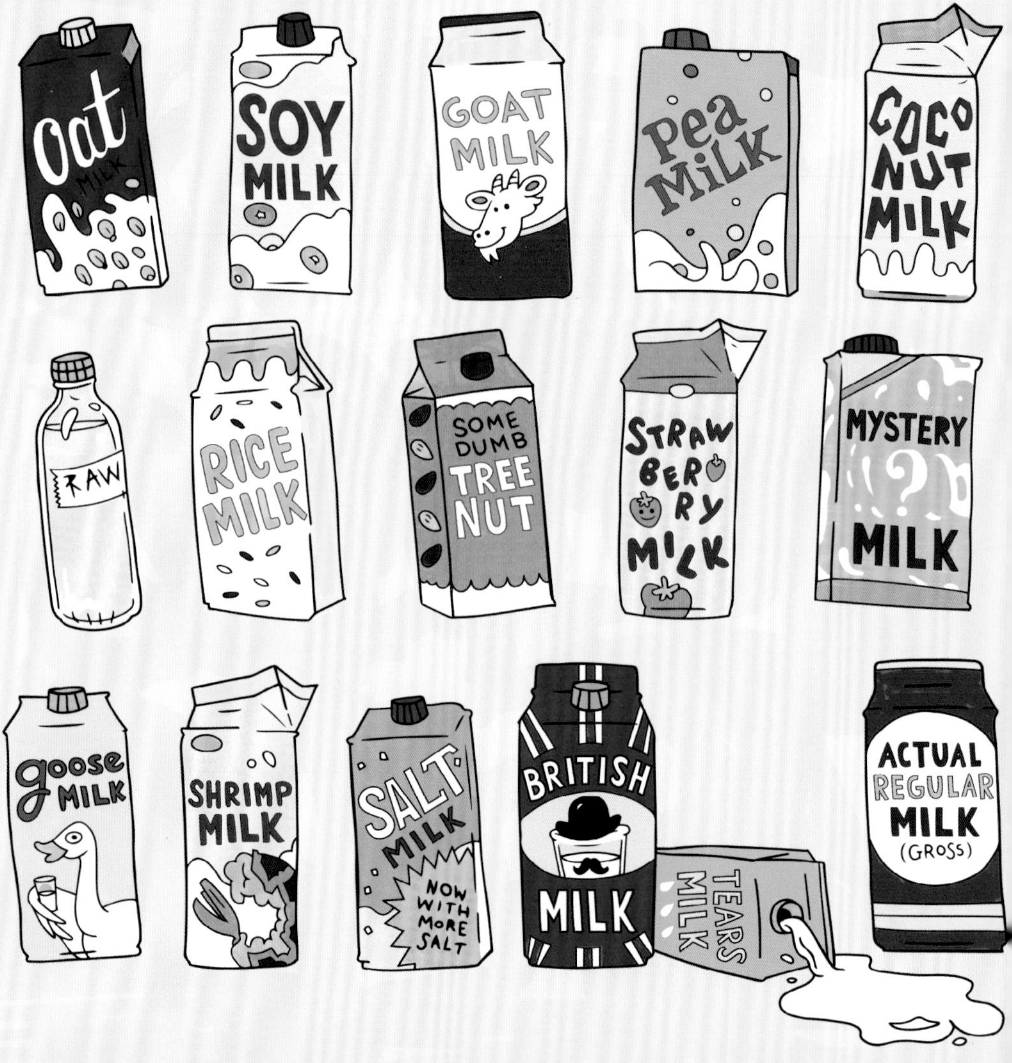
Oat MILK
SOY MILK
GOAT MILK
Pea Milk
COCO NUT MILK
RAW
RICE MILK
SOME DUMB TREE NUT
STRAW BER RY MILK
MYSTERY ? MILK
goose MILK
SHRIMP MILK
SALT MILK
NOW WITH MORE SALT
BRITISH MILK
TEARS MILK
ACTUAL REGULAR MILK (GROSS)

There are too many milks.

AND I'M ALLERGIC
TO ALL OF THEM!

Salads cost thirty dollars now.

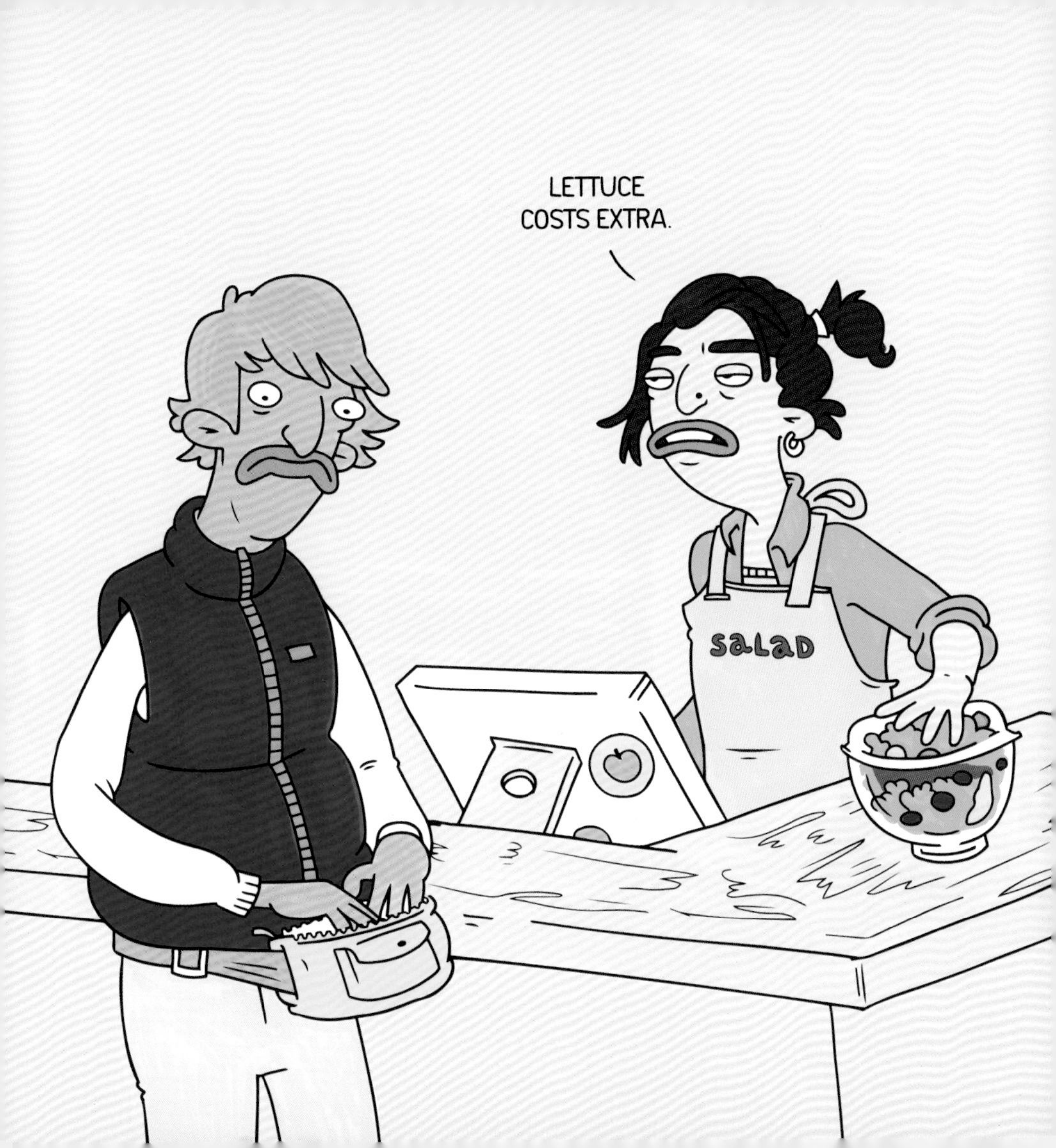
LETTUCE COSTS EXTRA.
SALAD

You'll always have a fork that doesn't match the other forks.

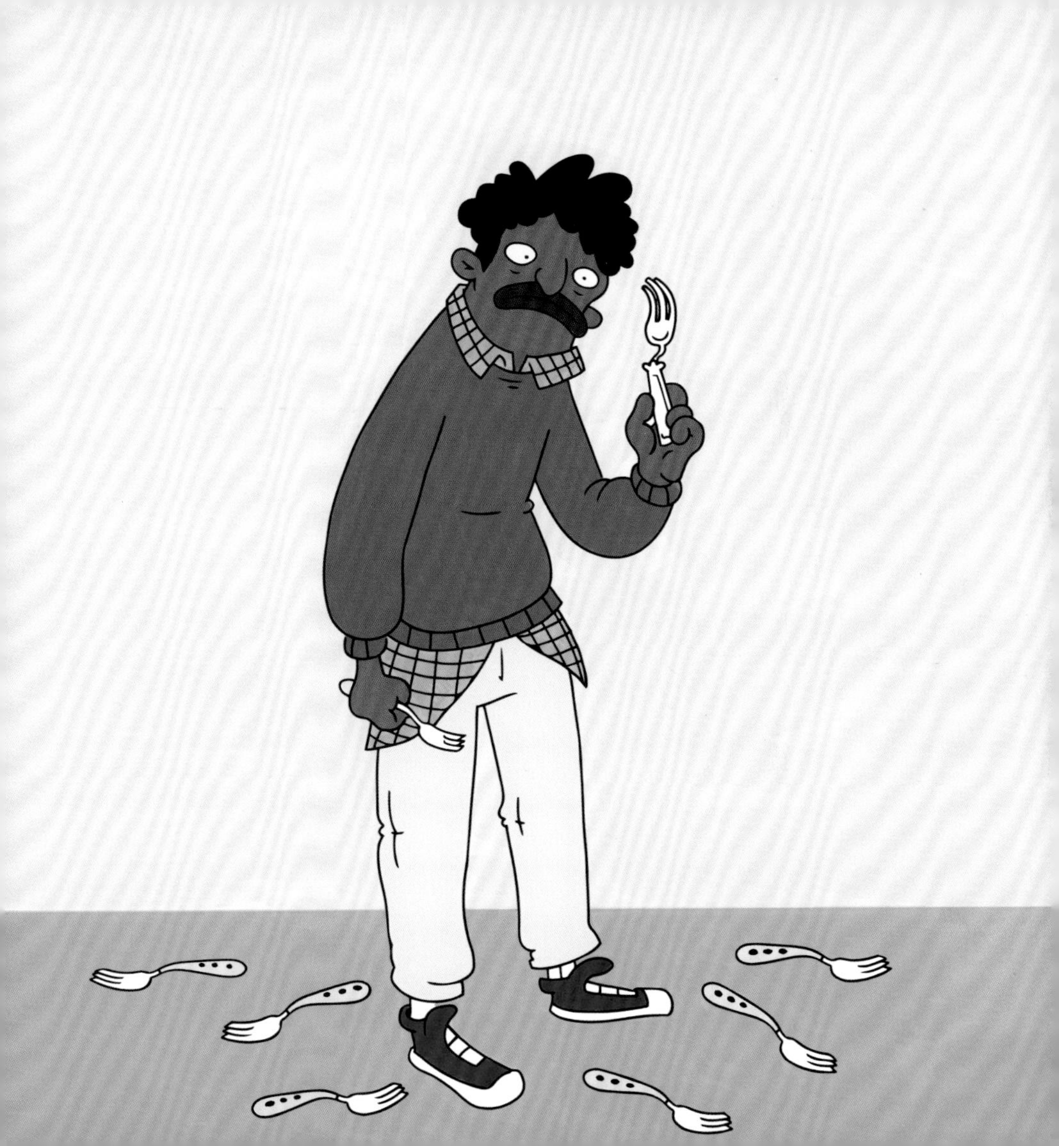

You have to be funny or interesting on, like, six different platforms.

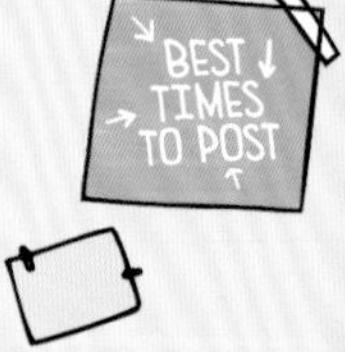
BEST TIMES TO POST

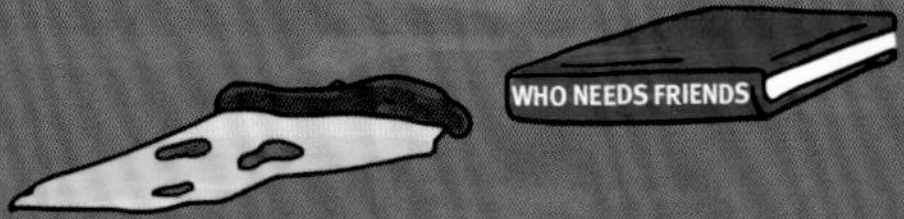
WHO NEEDS FRIENDS

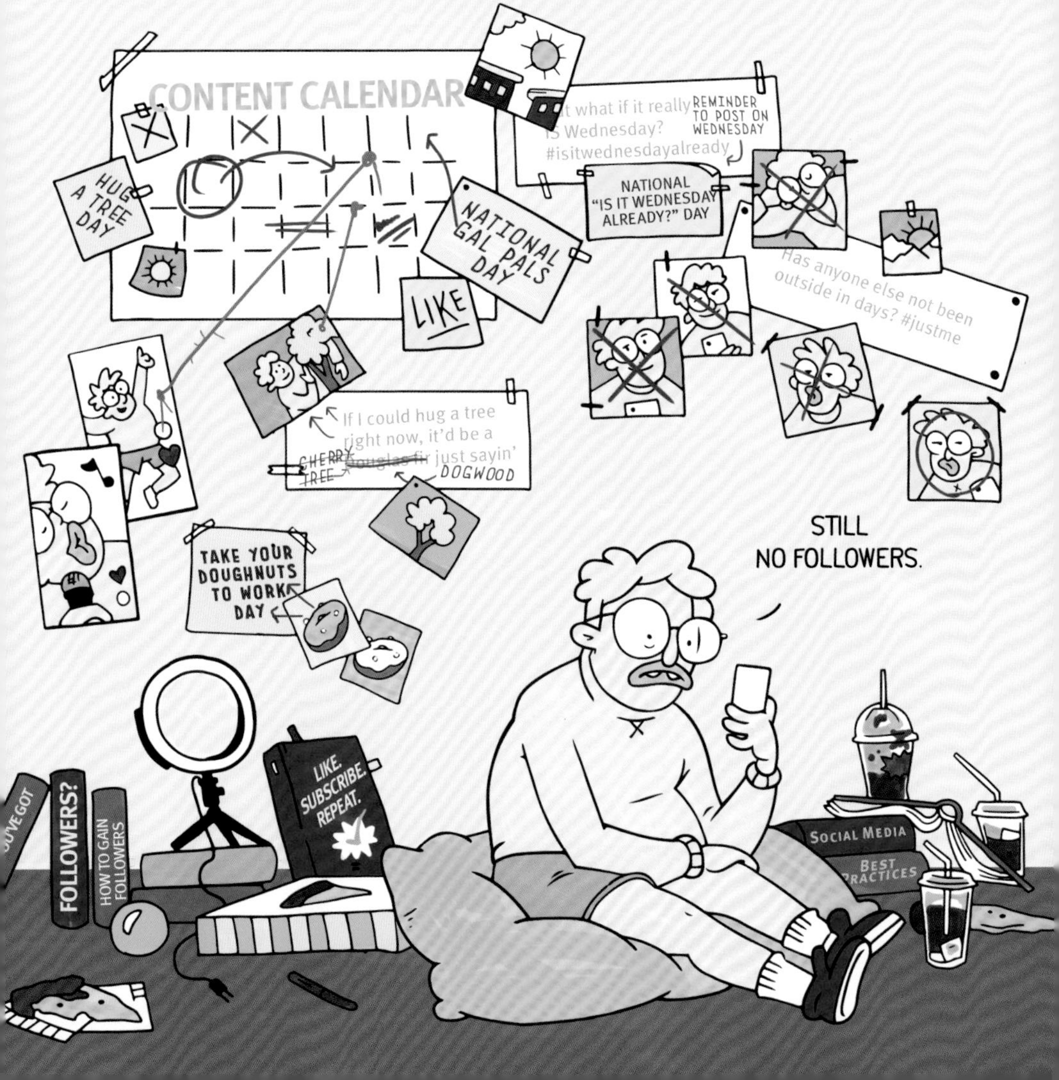
CONTENT CALENDAR
HUG A TREE DAY
NATIONAL GAL PALS DAY
LIKE
...t what if it really is Wednesday? #isitwednesdayalready
REMINDER TO POST ON WEDNESDAY
NATIONAL "IS IT WEDNESDAY ALREADY?" DAY
Has anyone else not been outside in days? #justme
If I could hug a tree right now, it'd be a Douglas fir just sayin'
CHERRY TREE
DOGWOOD
TAKE YOUR DOUGHNUTS TO WORK DAY
STILL NO FOLLOWERS.
FOLLOWERS?
HOW TO GAIN FOLLOWERS
LIKE. SUBSCRIBE. REPEAT.
SOCIAL MEDIA
BEST PRACTICES

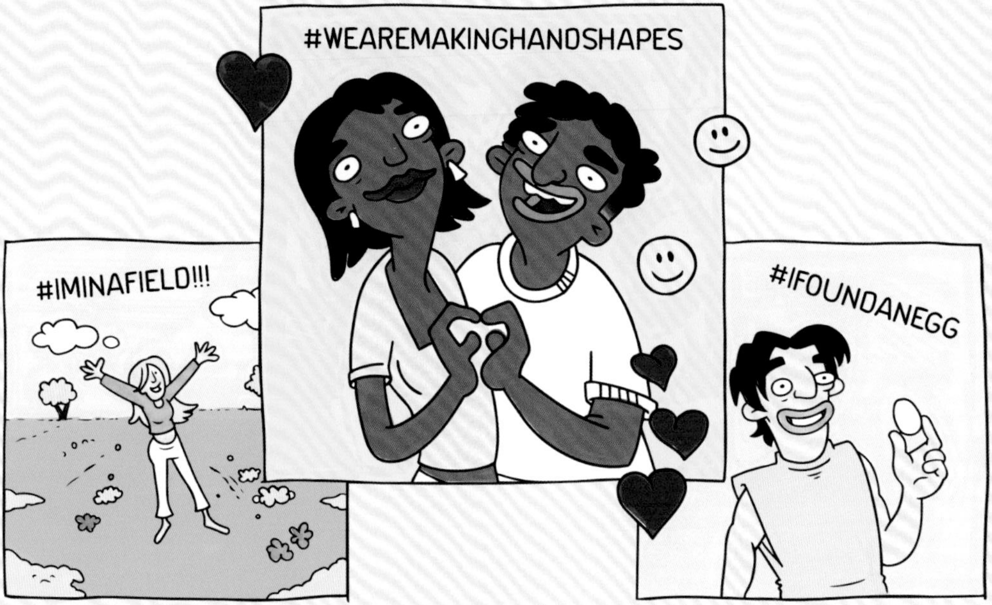
#IMINAFIELD!!!
#WEAREMAKINGHANDSHAPES
#IFOUNDANEGG

Everything's gotta be content.

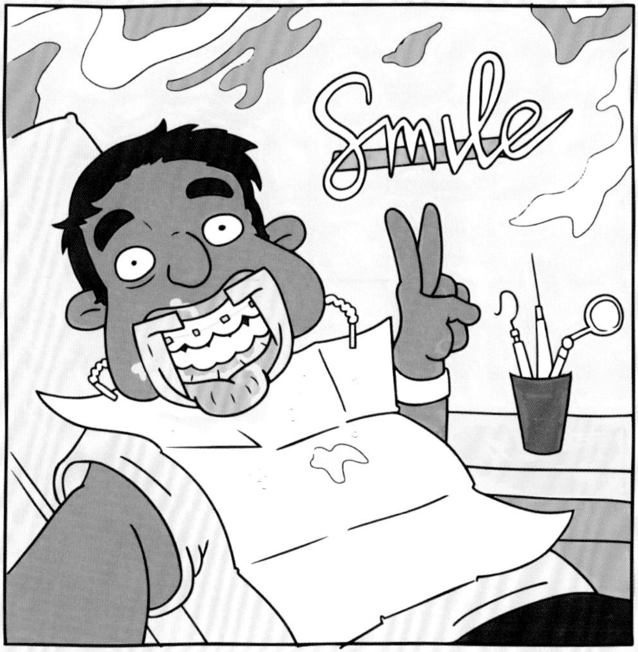
Smile

Even your dentist's office.

You have to figure out your
most attractive camera angles
like you're some kind of celebrity,
even though you're probably just some
regular person who maybe ate tuna
out of the can over the sink last night.

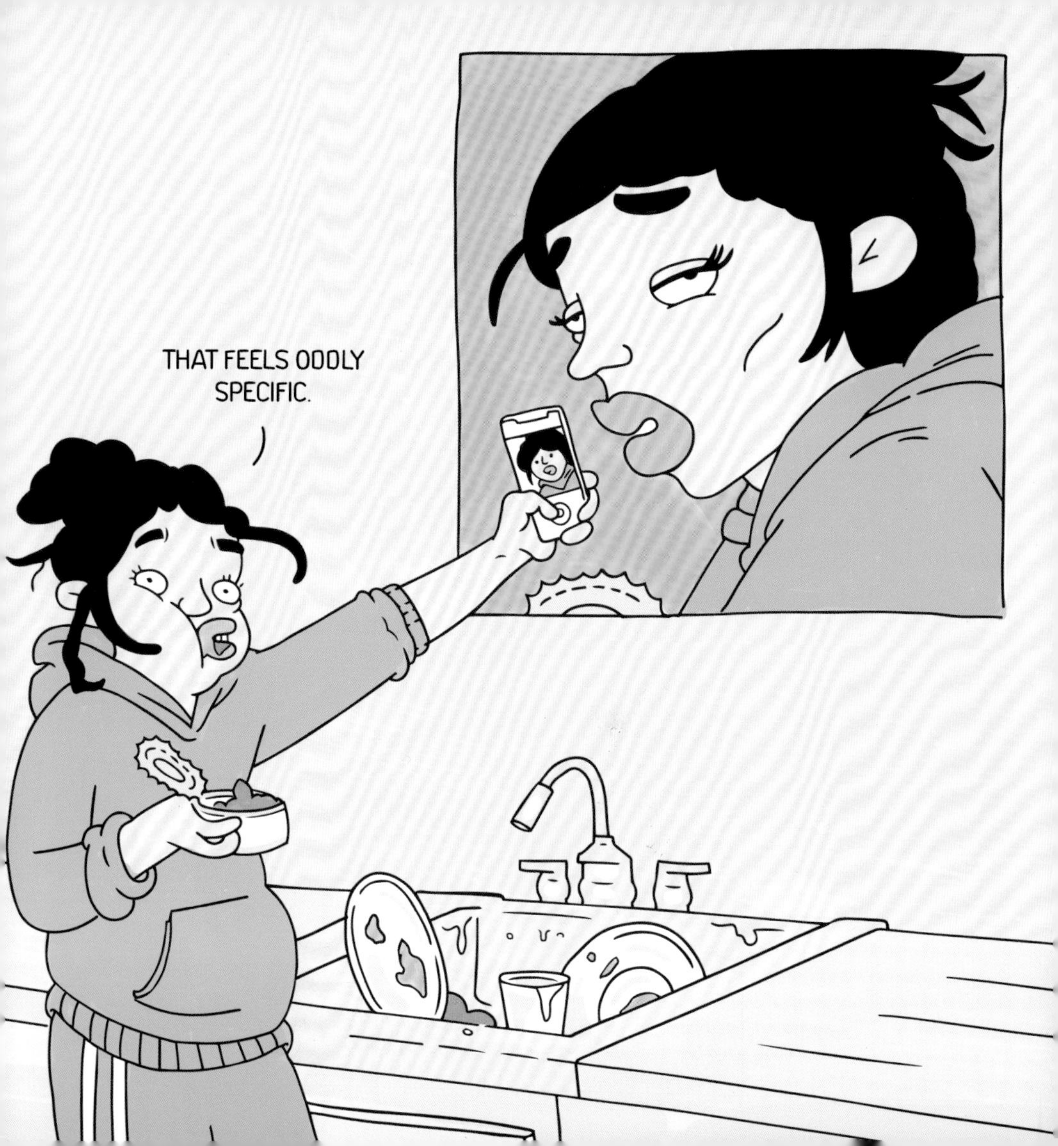
THAT FEELS ODDLY SPECIFIC.

These days, you have to swipe to find a person you are compatible with.

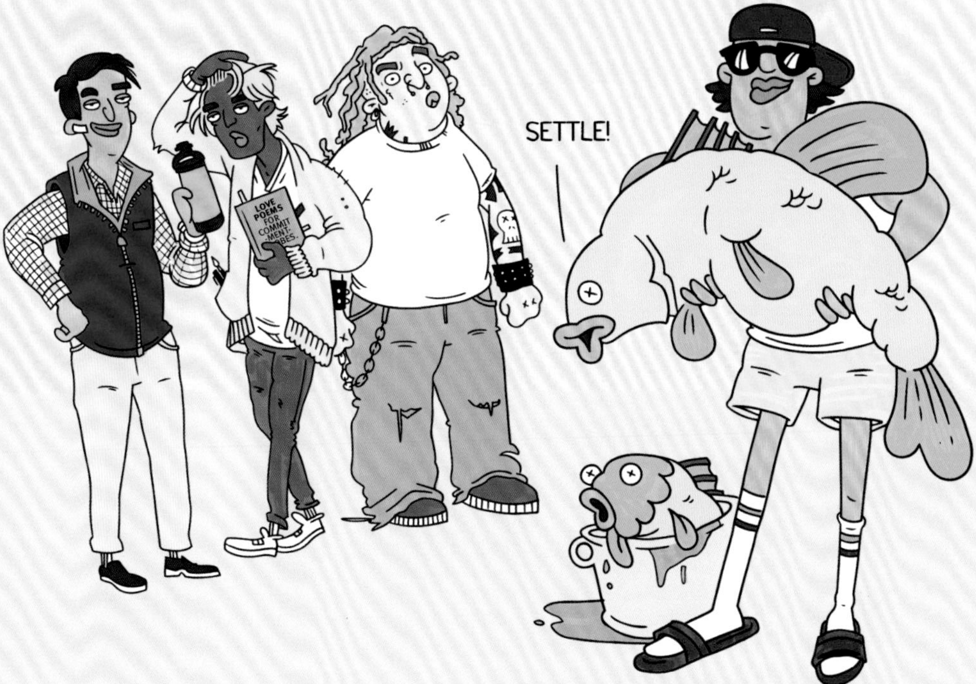
LOVE POEMS FOR COMMIT-MENT-
SETTLE!

Then you have to find a therapist you are compatible with to deal with the person you are compatible with.

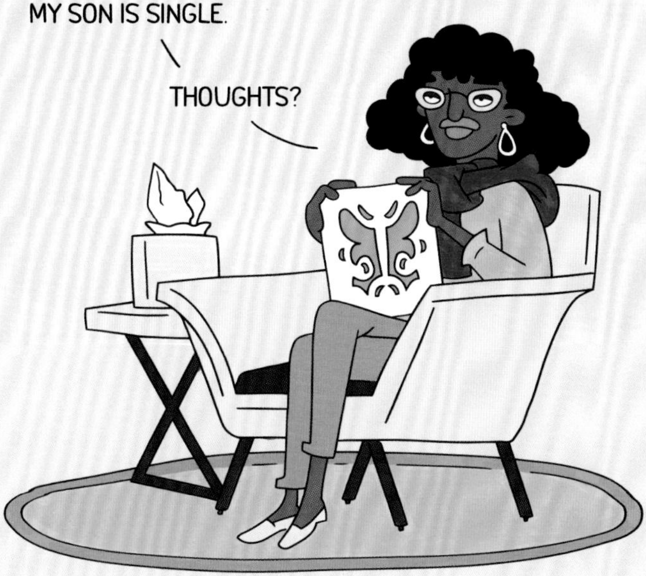
MY SON IS SINGLE.
THOUGHTS?

Your ex posts constantly.

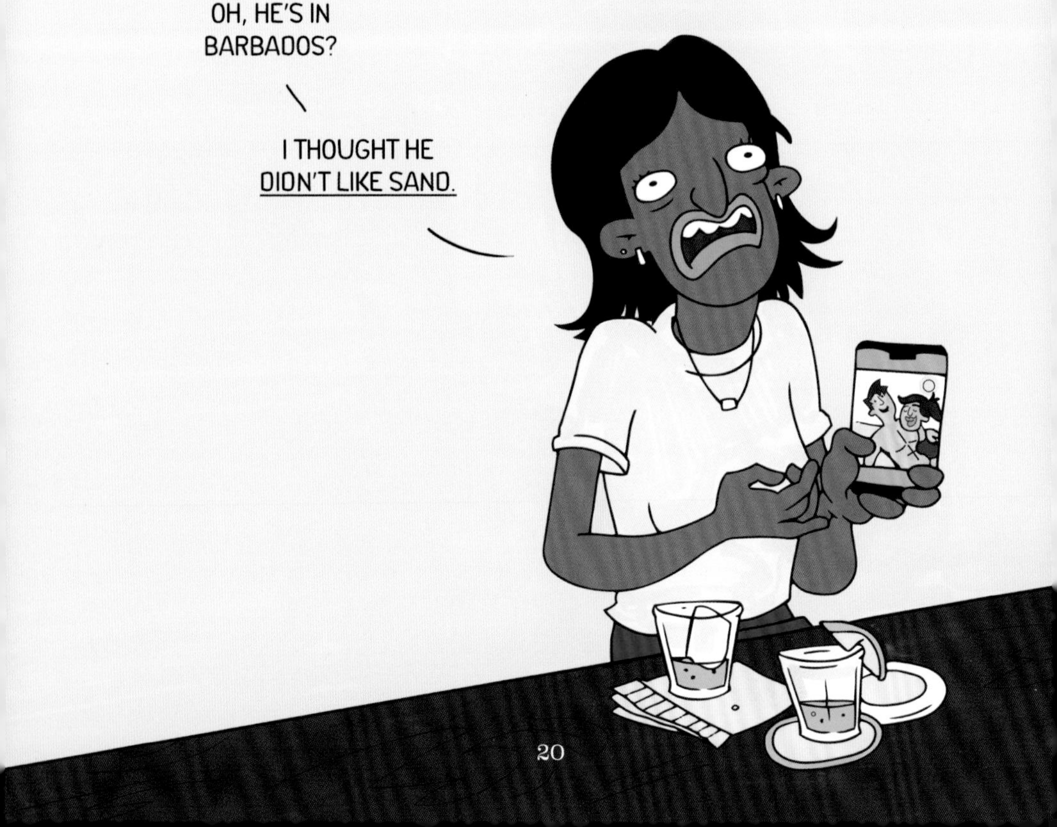

OH, HE'S IN BARBADOS?
I THOUGHT HE DIDN'T LIKE SAND.

Or your ex posts nothing.

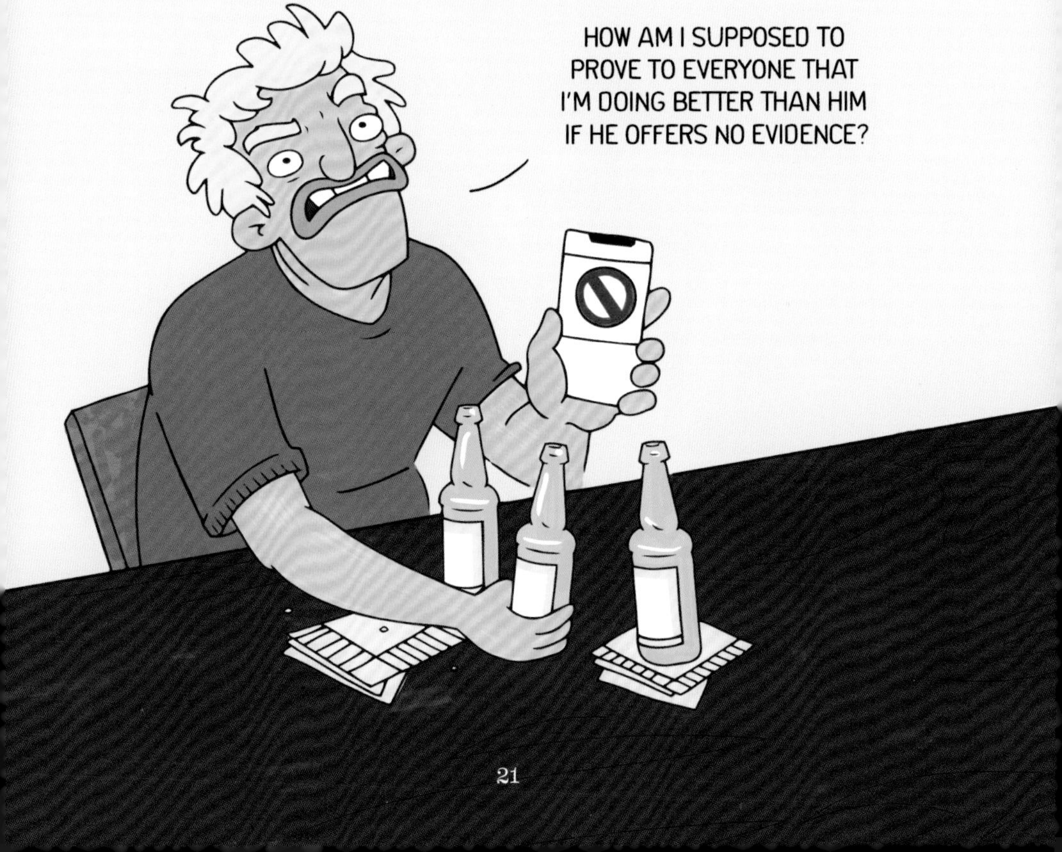
HOW AM I SUPPOSED TO PROVE TO EVERYONE THAT I'M DOING BETTER THAN HIM IF HE OFFERS NO EVIDENCE?

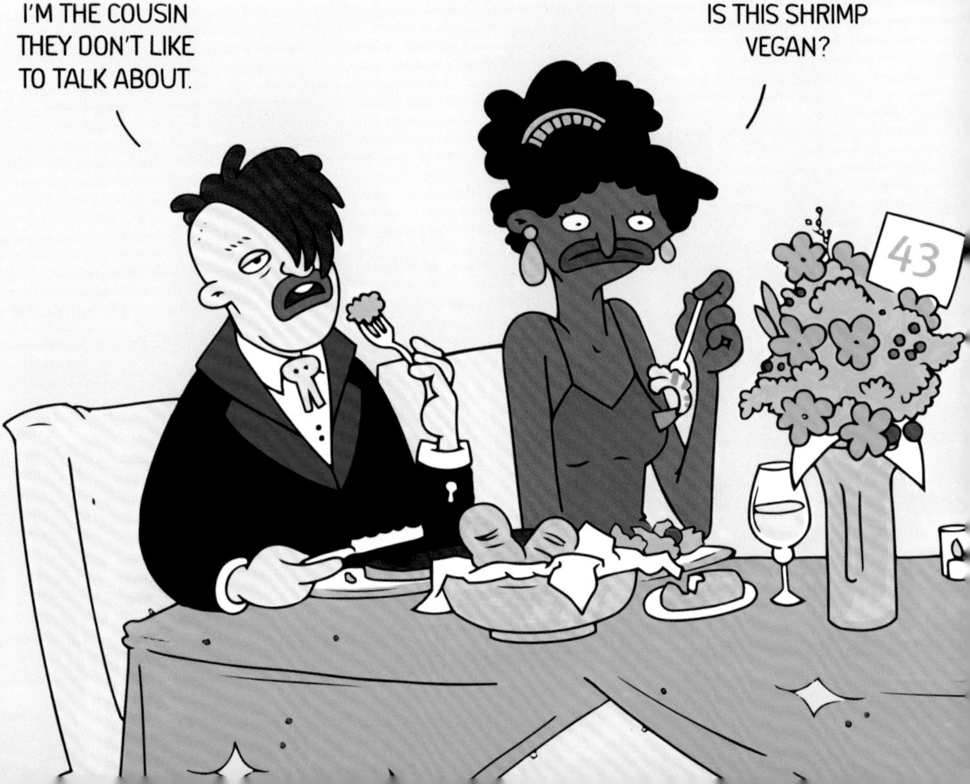
I'M THE COUSIN THEY DON'T LIKE TO TALK ABOUT.
IS THIS SHRIMP VEGAN?
43

Sometimes you will be invited to weddings.

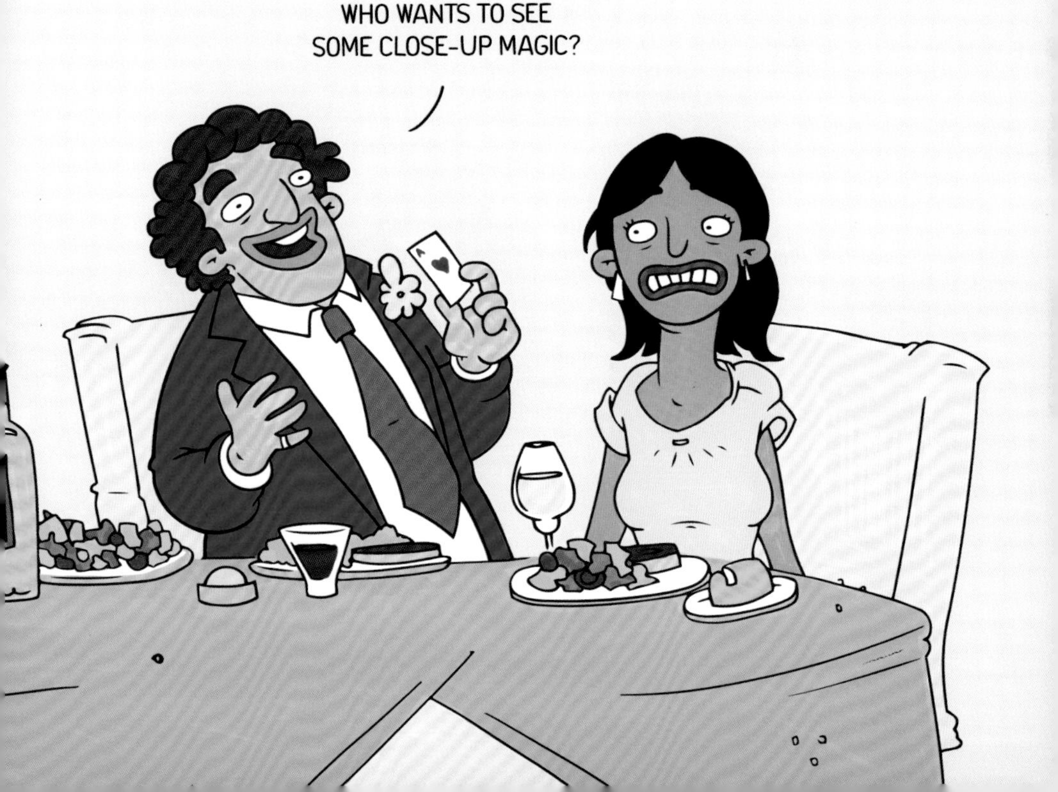
WHO WANTS TO SEE
SOME CLOSE-UP MAGIC?

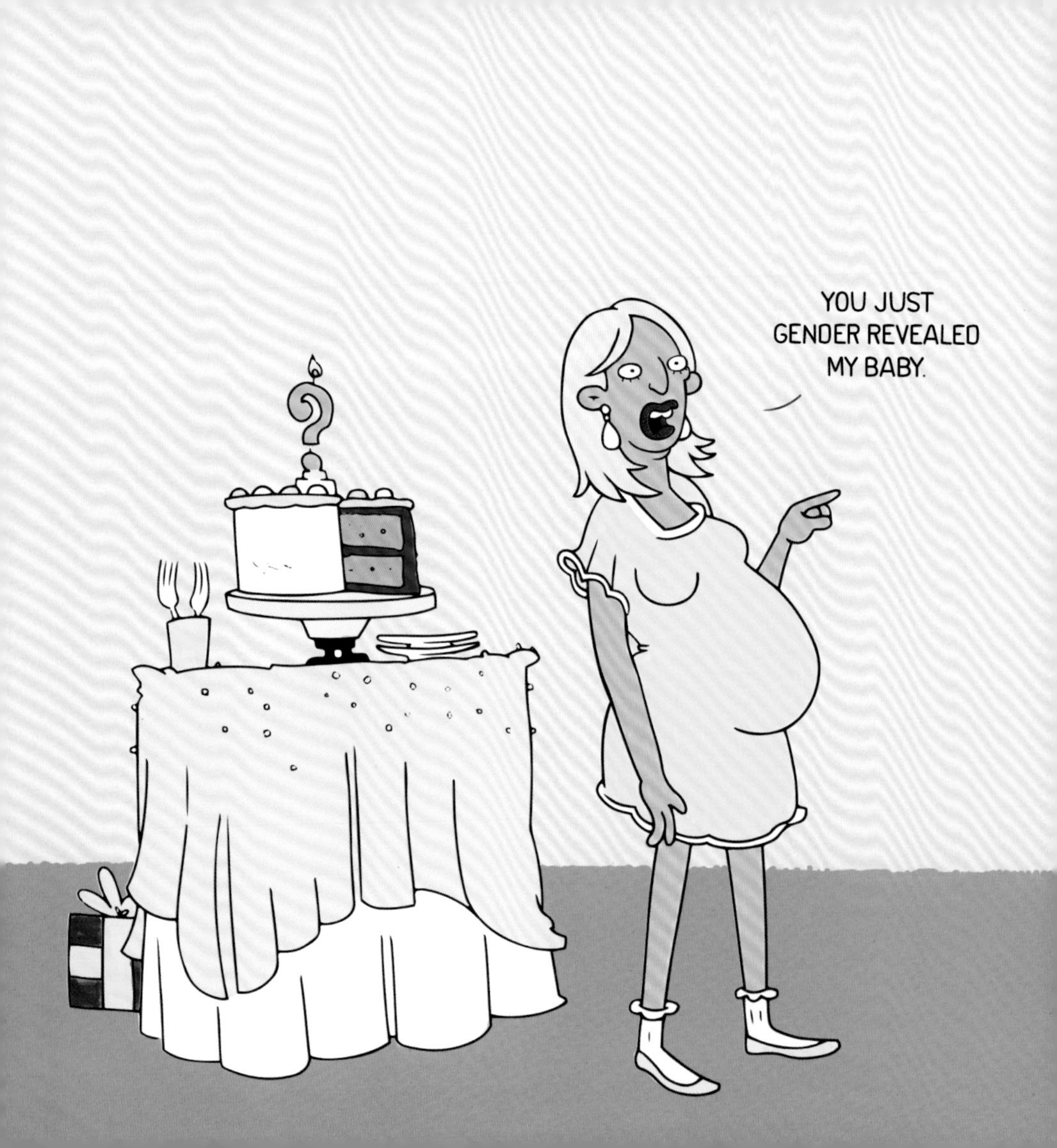
YOU JUST
GENDER REVEALED
MY BABY.

Sometimes you will be invited
to baby showers.

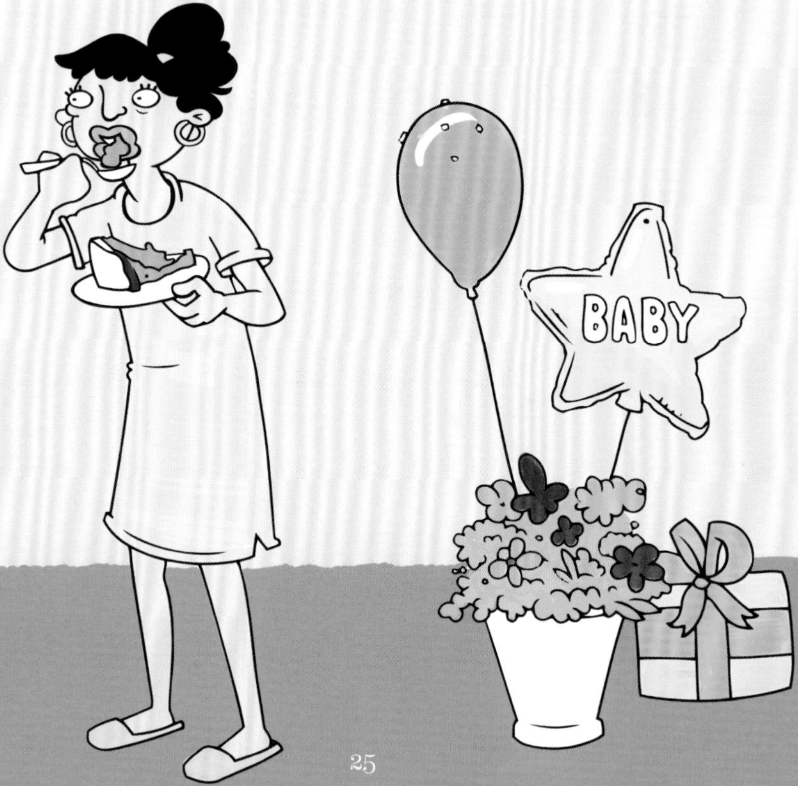
BABY

Sometimes you will be invited to . . .
whatever this is.

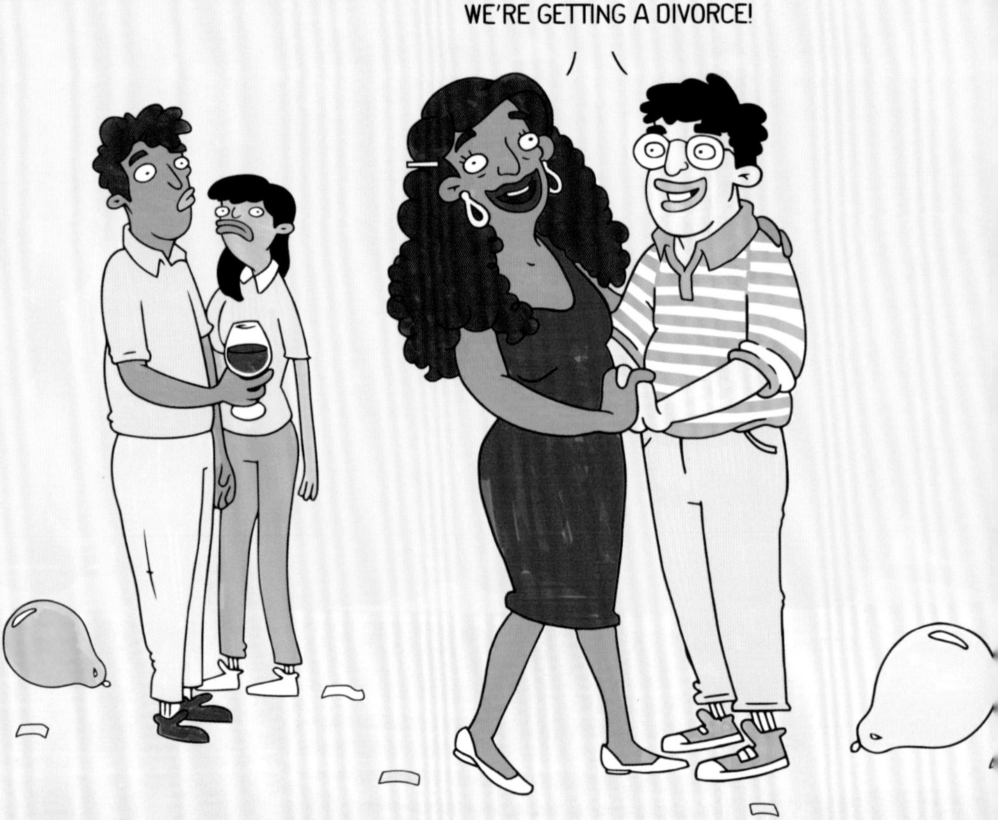
WE'RE GETTING A DIVORCE!

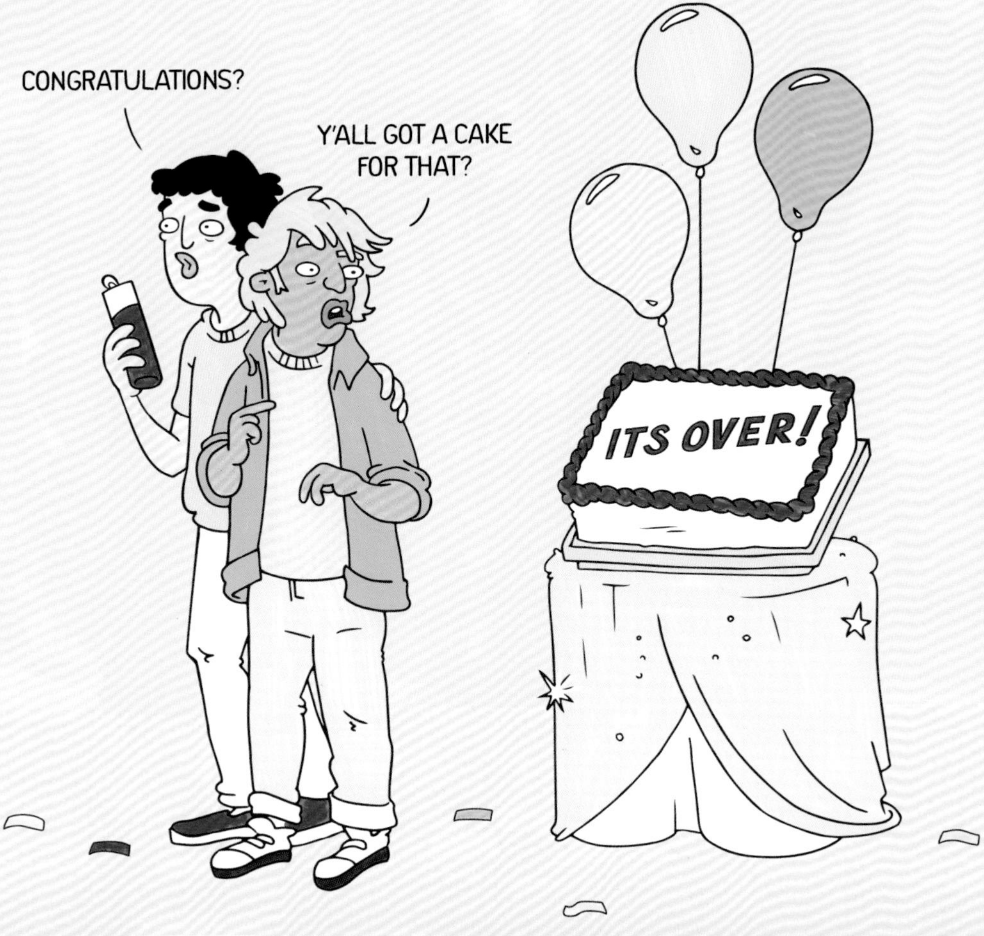
CONGRATULATIONS?
Y'ALL GOT A CAKE FOR THAT?
ITS OVER!

We haven't figured out a better solution to the whole woman-taking-the-man's-last-name thing.

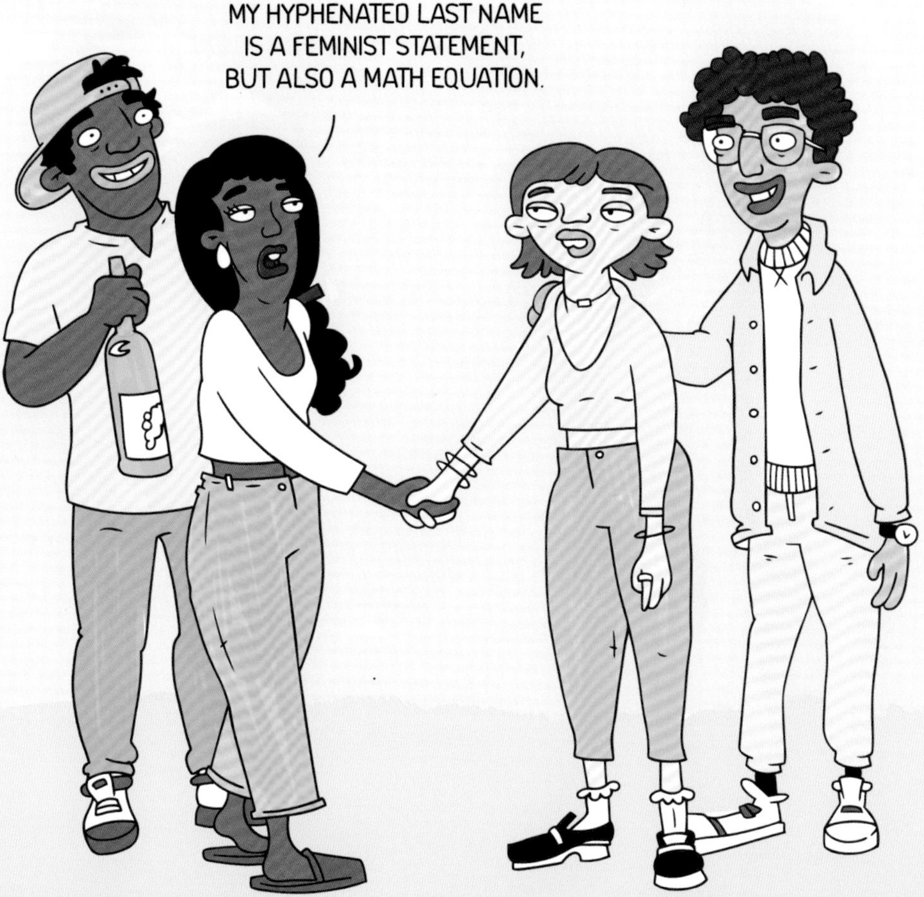
MY HYPHENATED LAST NAME IS A FEMINIST STATEMENT, BUT ALSO A MATH EQUATION.

Sometimes you will have to hang out with people you don't really like.

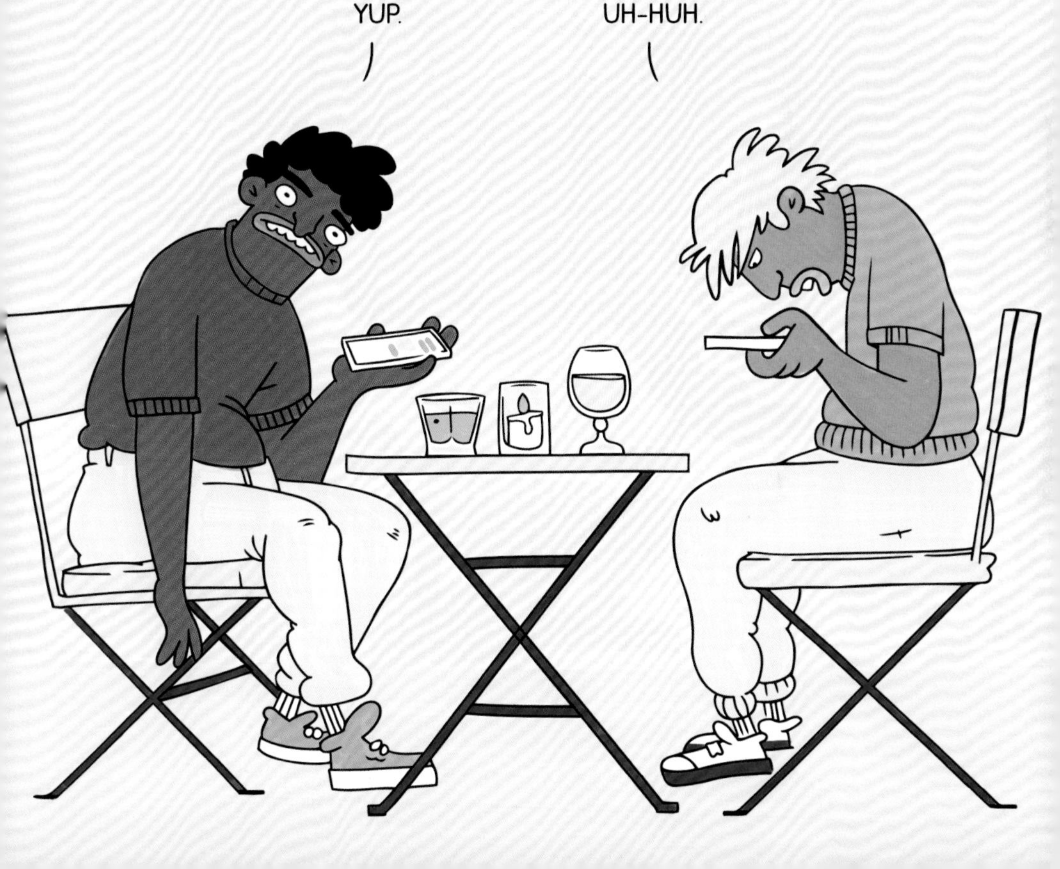
YUP.
UH-HUH.

Sometimes you will have to hang out
with people you don't really like who also
decide how much money you make.

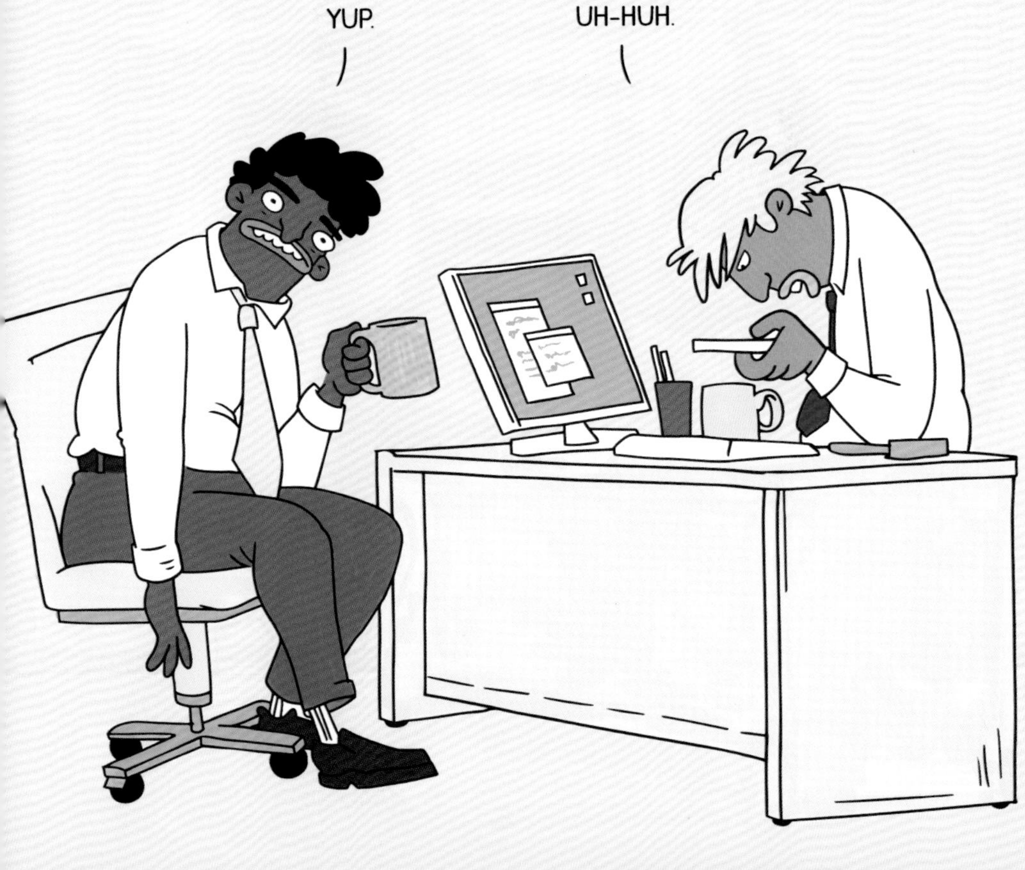
YUP.
UH-HUH.

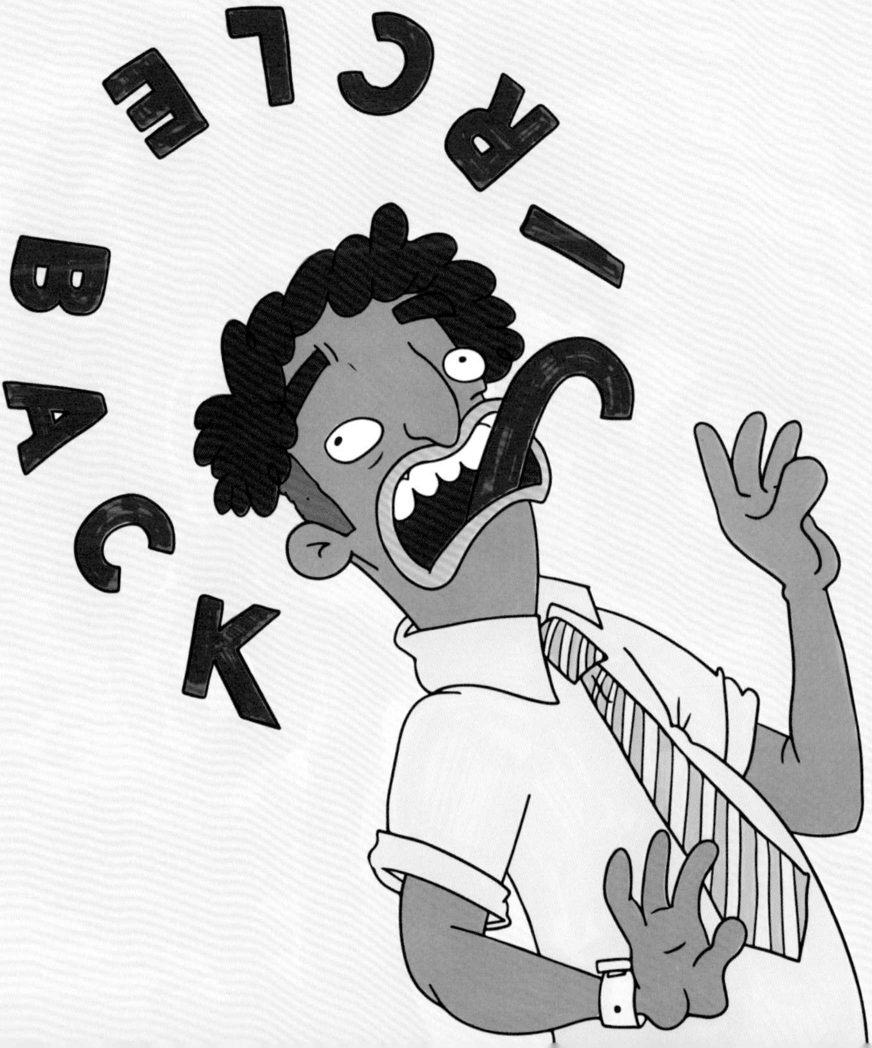
CIRCLE BACK

There will be a day when you say "circle back" in complete sincerity.

It's sooner than you think.

kindly! → THIS CITY IS GOING TO EAT ME ALIVE.

cheers → I STUDIED ABROAD ONCE.

regards! → MY FAVORITE MOVIE IS STILL *TITANIC*.

-r → I OWN THE COMPANY AND YOU ONLY NEED MY FIRST INITIAL TO FEEL MY POWER.

TYSM → GOOGLE IT.

thanks, → NORMAL THANKS.

thanks! → I'M A SUBMISSIVE TO LATE-STAGE CAPITALISM.

thanks!!!! → I HAVE RECENTLY GOTTEN VERY INTO NITRO COLD BREW!!!!

thanks. → FUCK YOU.

You have to decide which kind of
email sign-off person you are.

And yes. It matters.

Sometimes people wear similar outfits.

Just be cool about it.

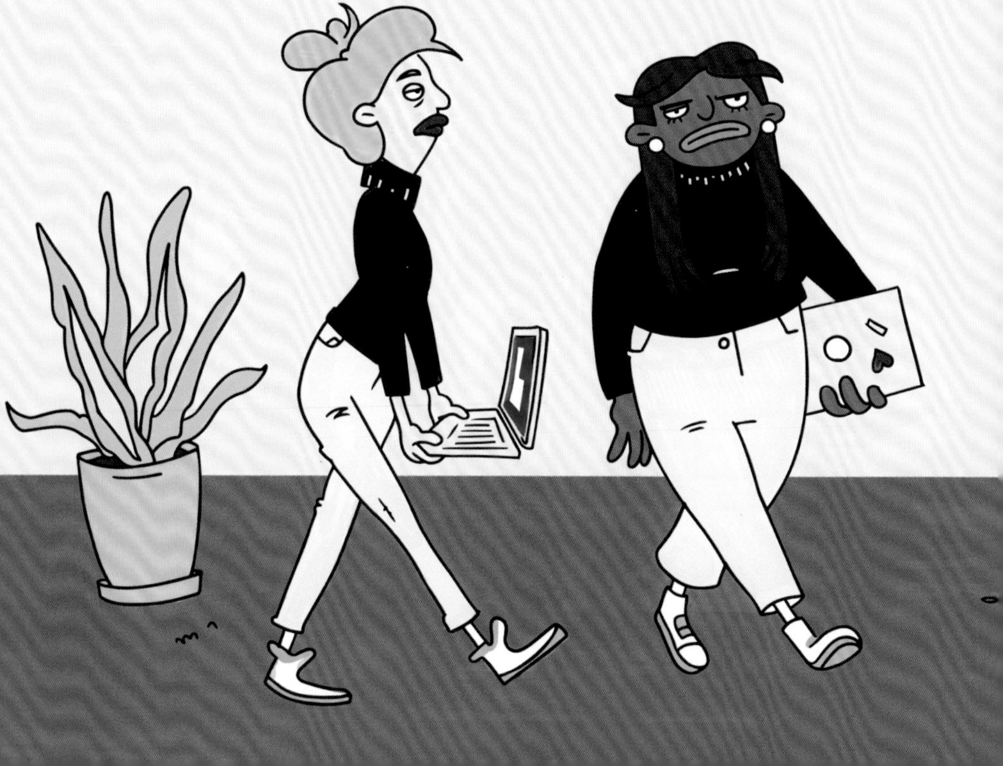

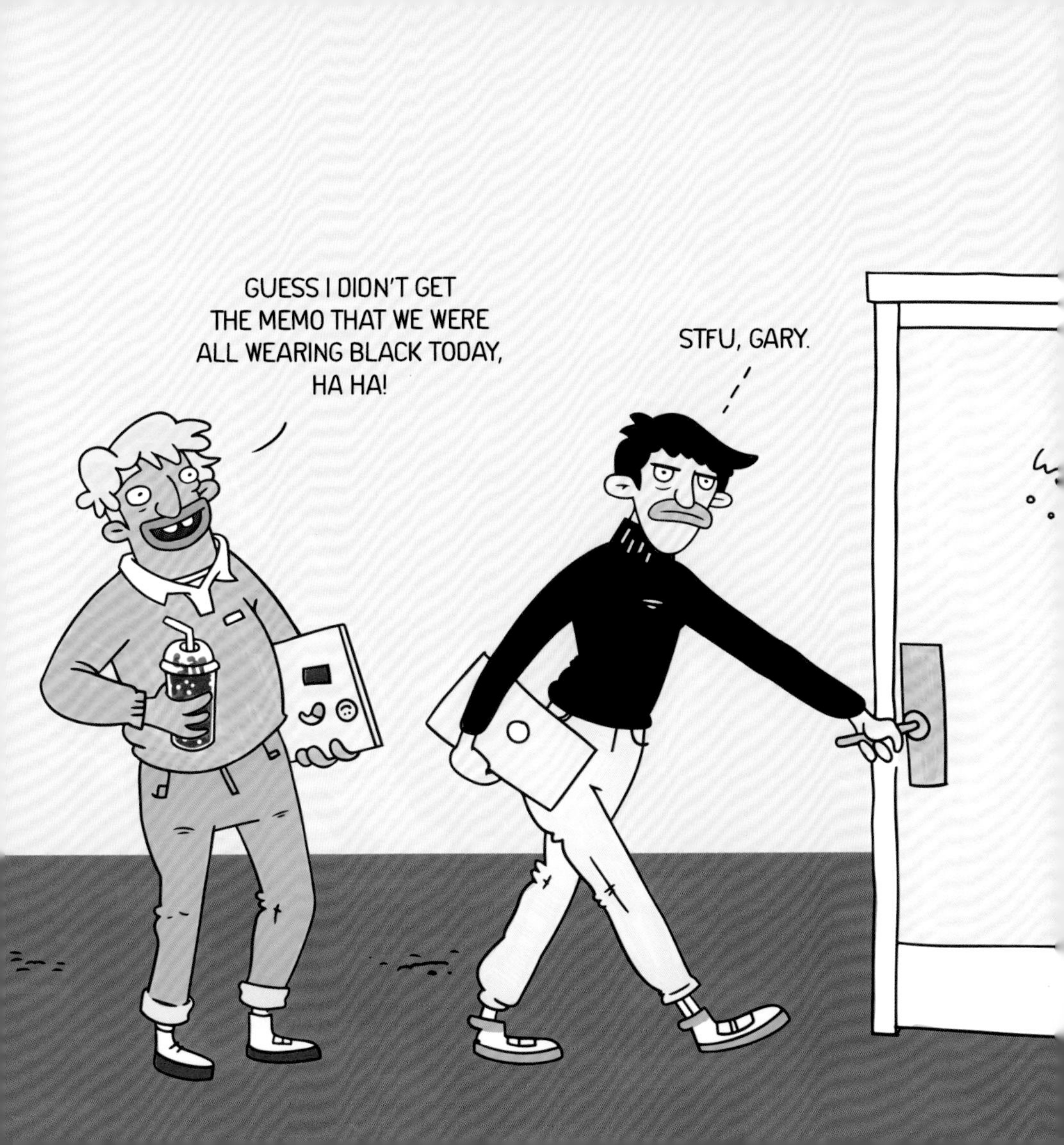
GUESS I DIDN'T GET THE MEMO THAT WE WERE ALL WEARING BLACK TODAY, HA HA!
STFU, GARY.

You have to work almost every day, and one day someone will call you "ma'am."

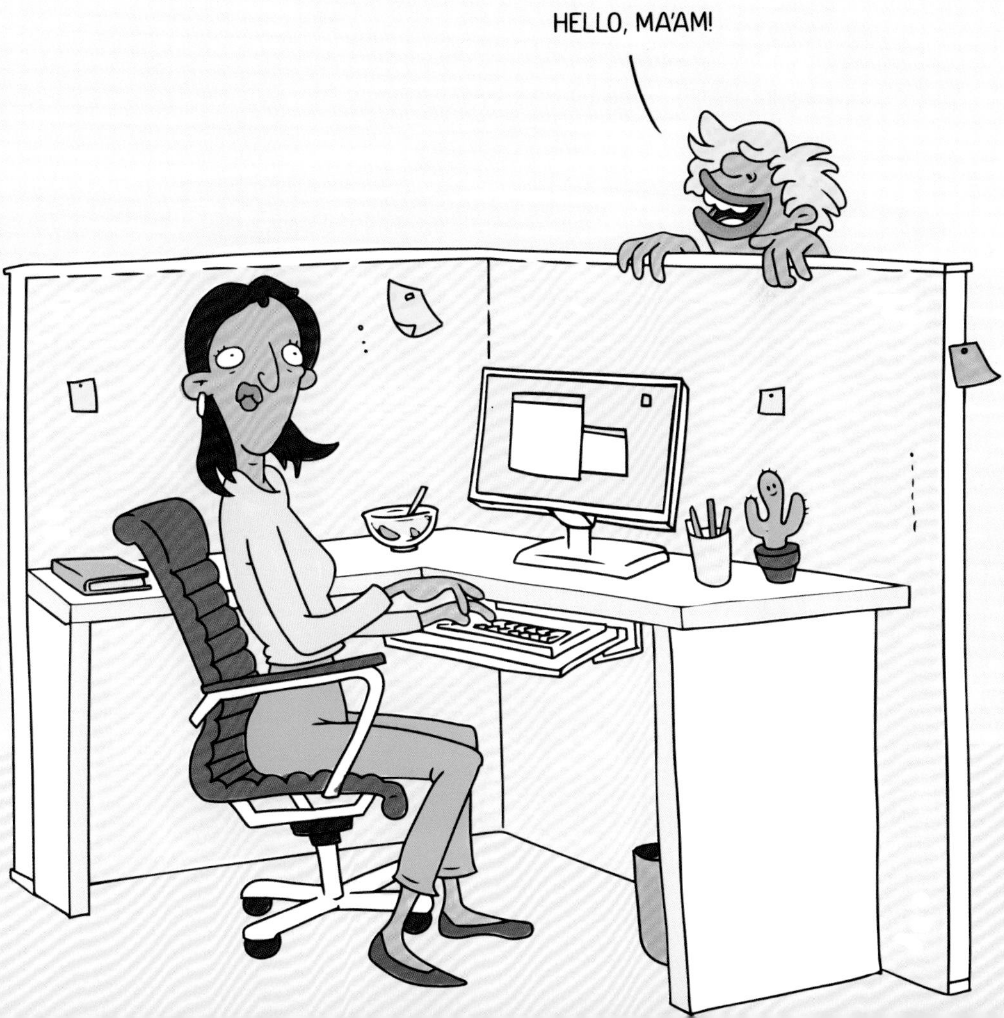
HELLO, MA'AM!

And you'll have to save up for Botox.

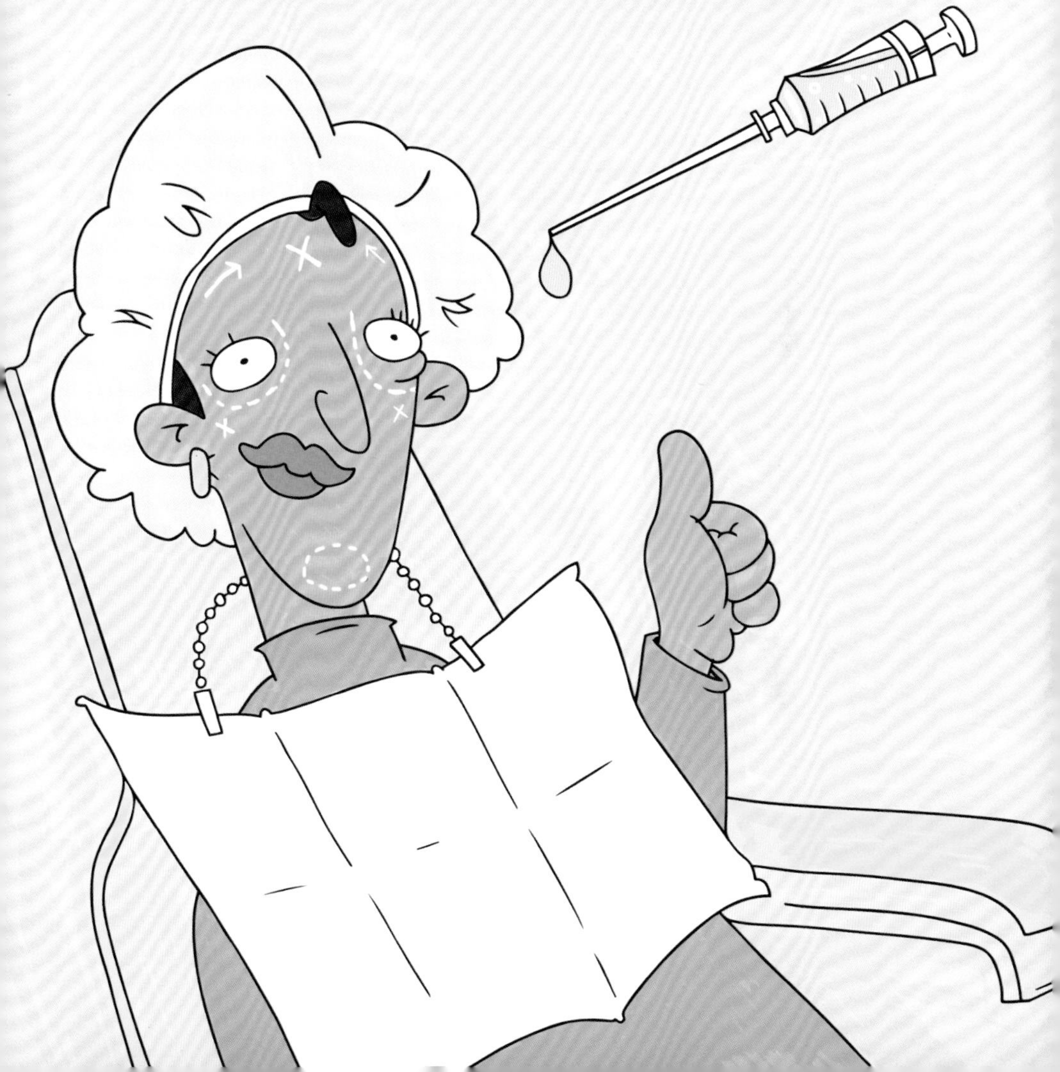

Your preferred sleeping position?

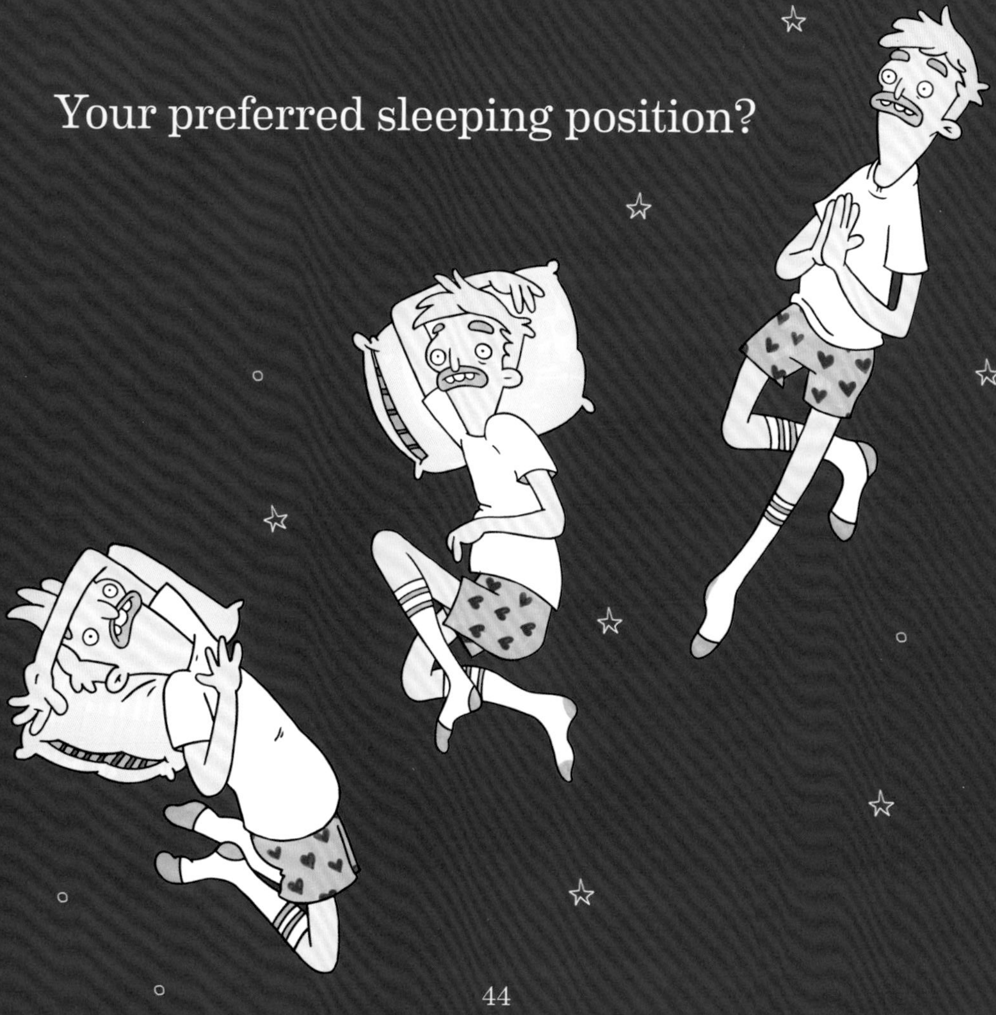

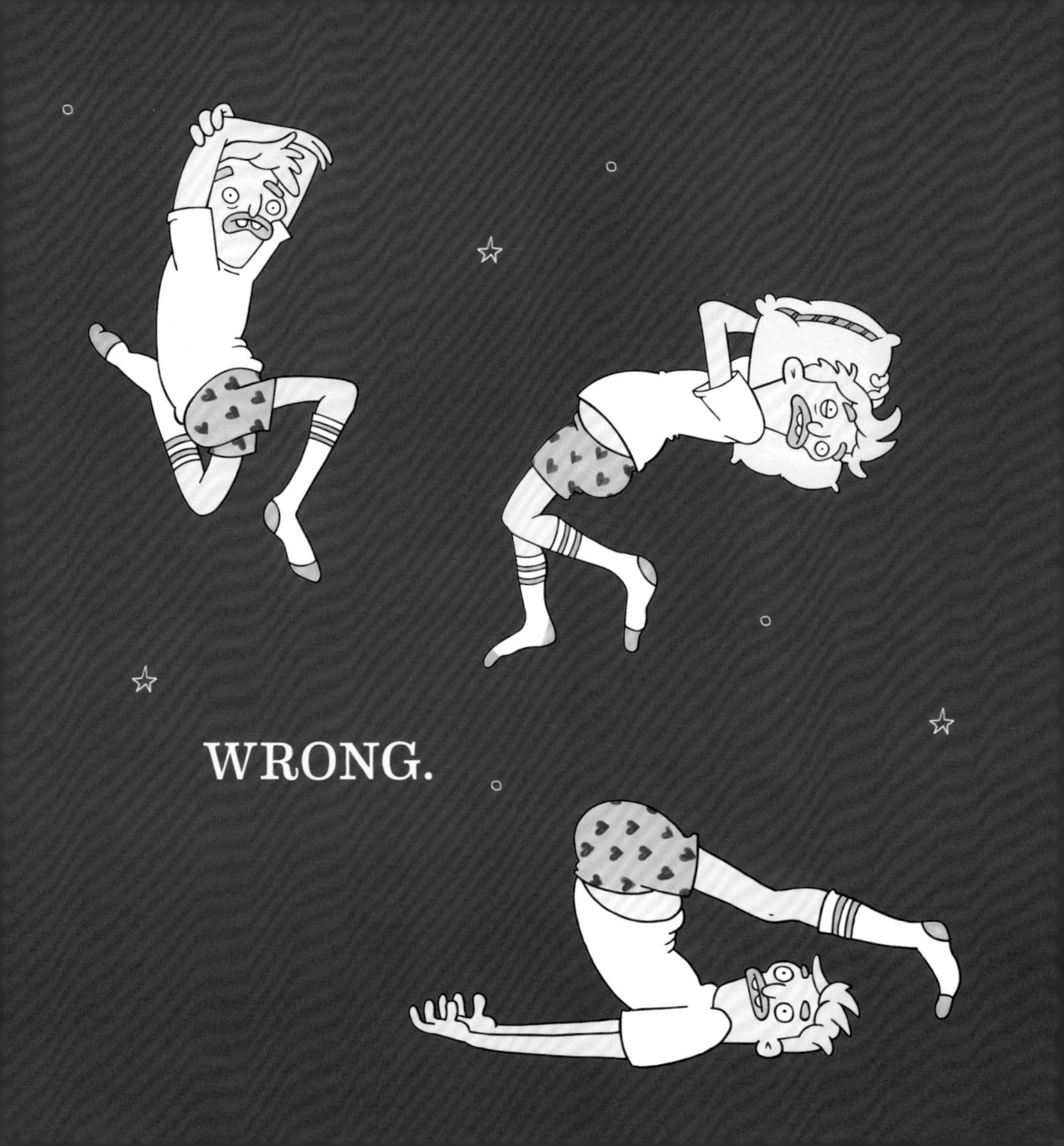
WRONG.

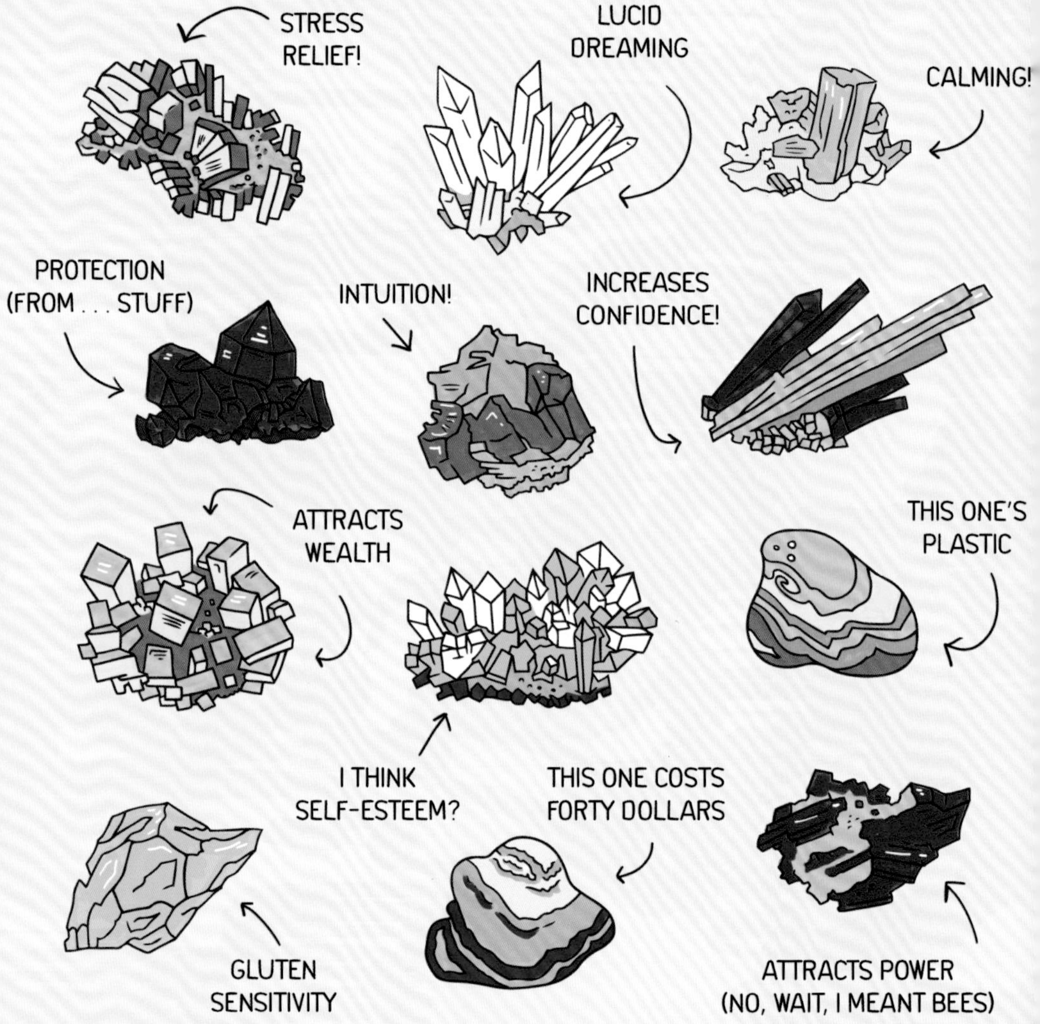
STRESS RELIEF!
LUCID DREAMING
CALMING!
PROTECTION (FROM . . . STUFF)
INTUITION!
INCREASES CONFIDENCE!
ATTRACTS WEALTH
THIS ONE'S PLASTIC
I THINK SELF-ESTEEM?
THIS ONE COSTS FORTY DOLLARS
GLUTEN SENSITIVITY
ATTRACTS POWER (NO, WAIT, I MEANT BEES)

But at least rocks have powers now.

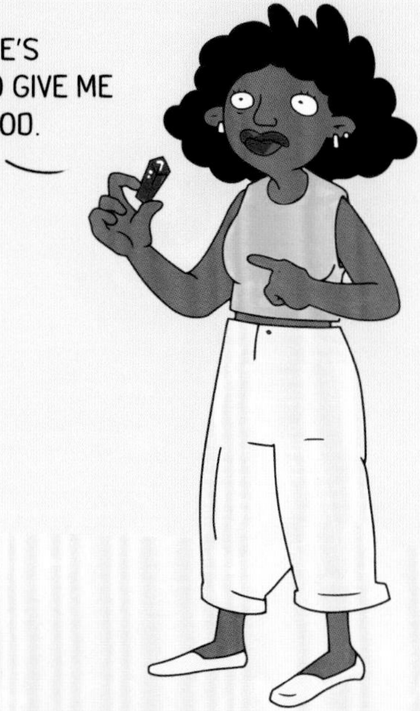
THIS ONE'S SUPPOSED TO GIVE ME MY PERIOD.

So do smells.

BUT I SPENT ALL
MY MONEY ON
MY PERIOD ROCK.

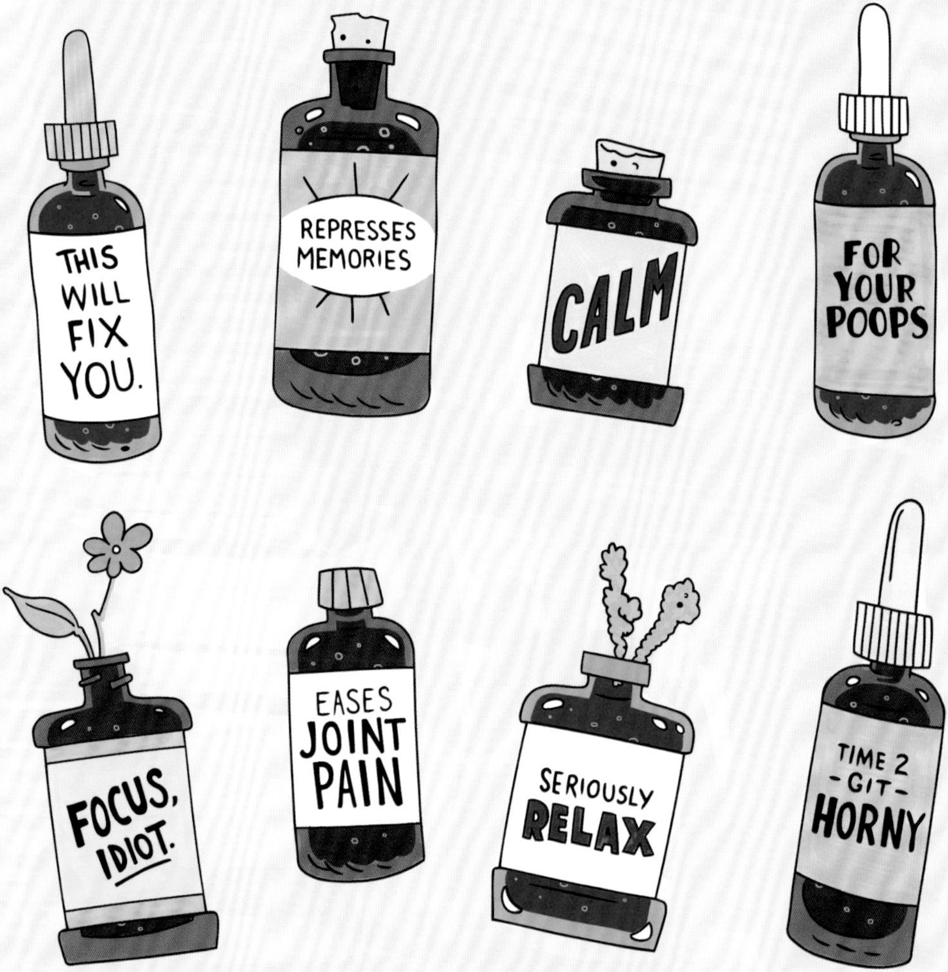
THIS WILL FIX YOU.
REPRESSES MEMORIES
CALM
FOR YOUR POOPS
FOCUS, IDIOT.
EASES JOINT PAIN
SERIOUSLY RELAX
TIME 2 -GIT- HORNY

Baths are now "experiences."

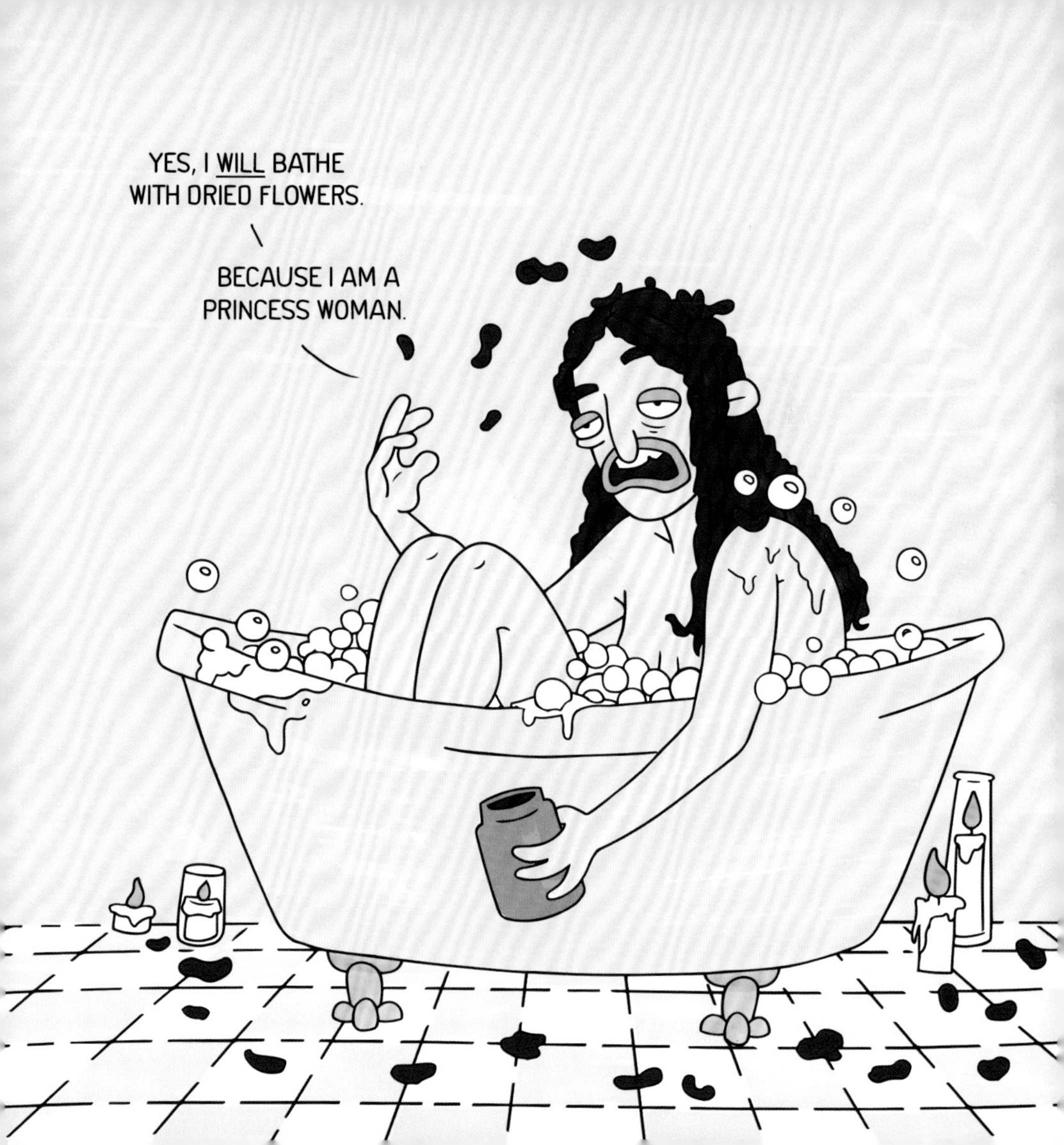
YES, I WILL BATHE WITH DRIED FLOWERS.
BECAUSE I AM A PRINCESS WOMAN.

Meditation has gotten very aggressive.

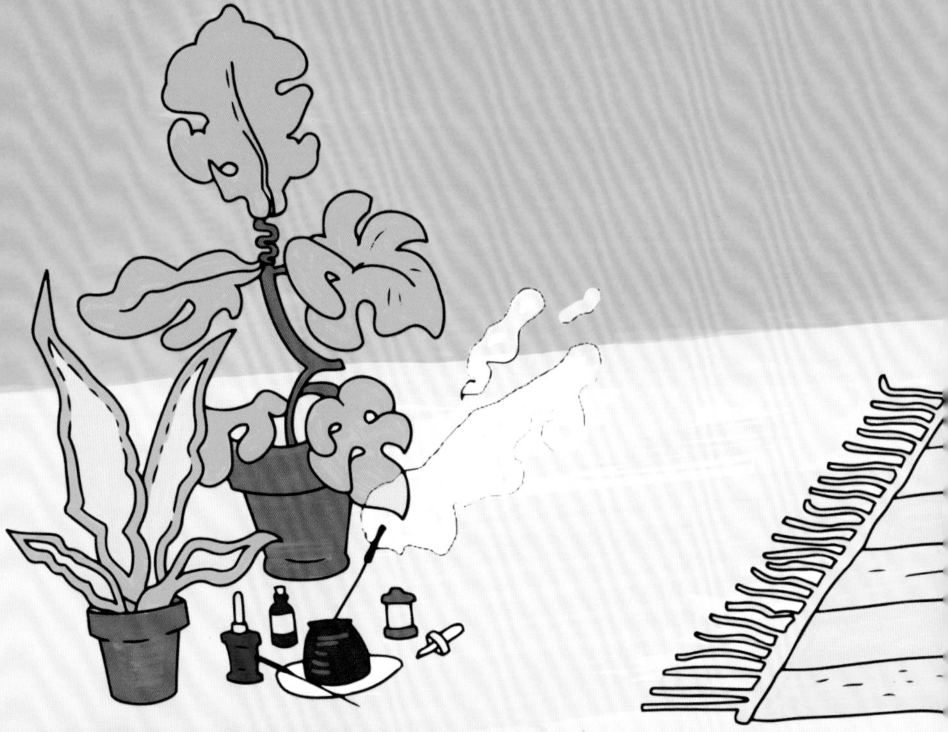

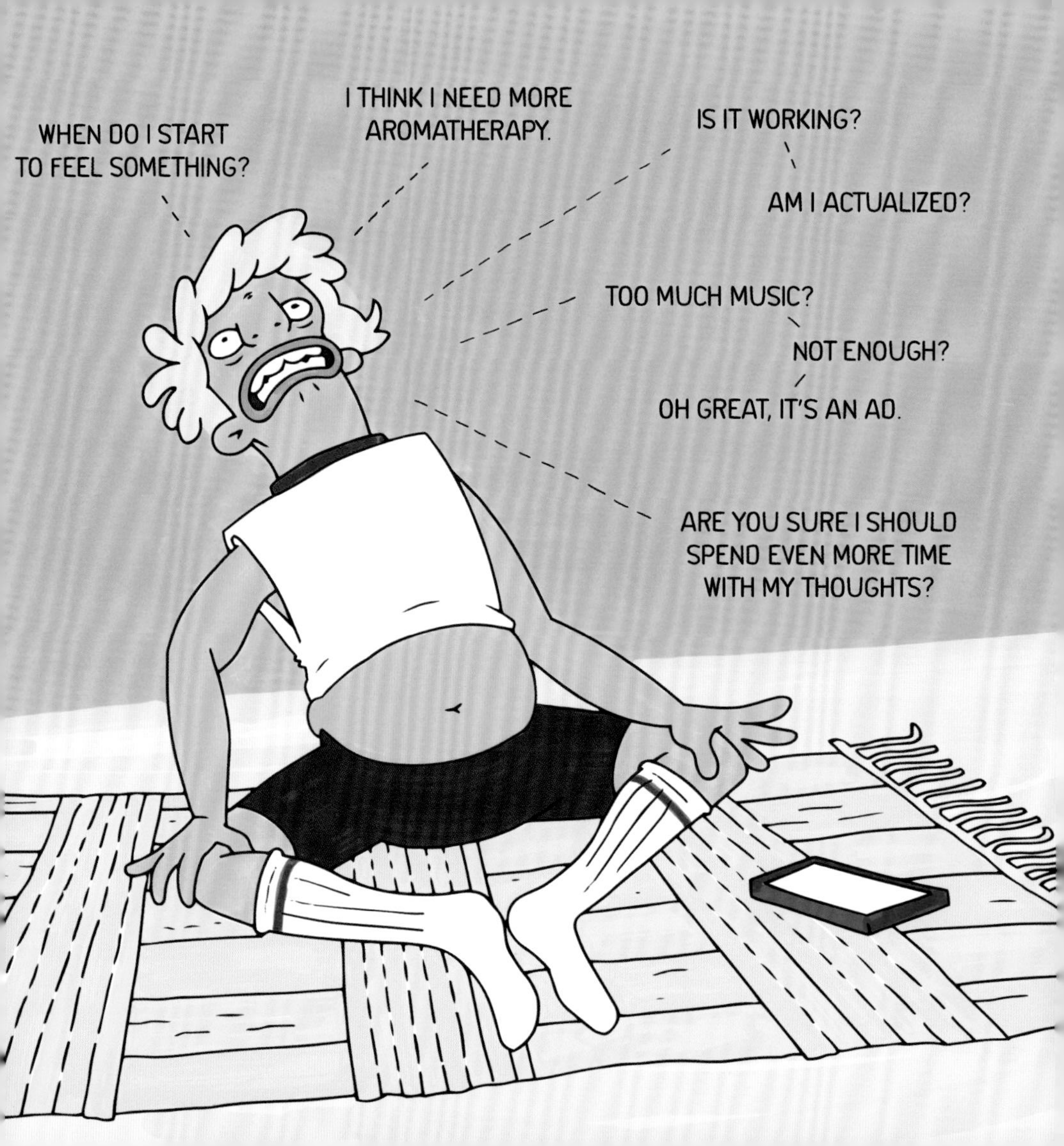
WHEN DO I START TO FEEL SOMETHING?
I THINK I NEED MORE AROMATHERAPY.
IS IT WORKING?
AM I ACTUALIZED?
TOO MUCH MUSIC?
NOT ENOUGH?
OH GREAT, IT'S AN AD.
ARE YOU SURE I SHOULD SPEND EVEN MORE TIME WITH MY THOUGHTS?

Motivational social media accounts
send really mixed messages.

Are we doing the body-positive thing
or are we intermittent fasting?

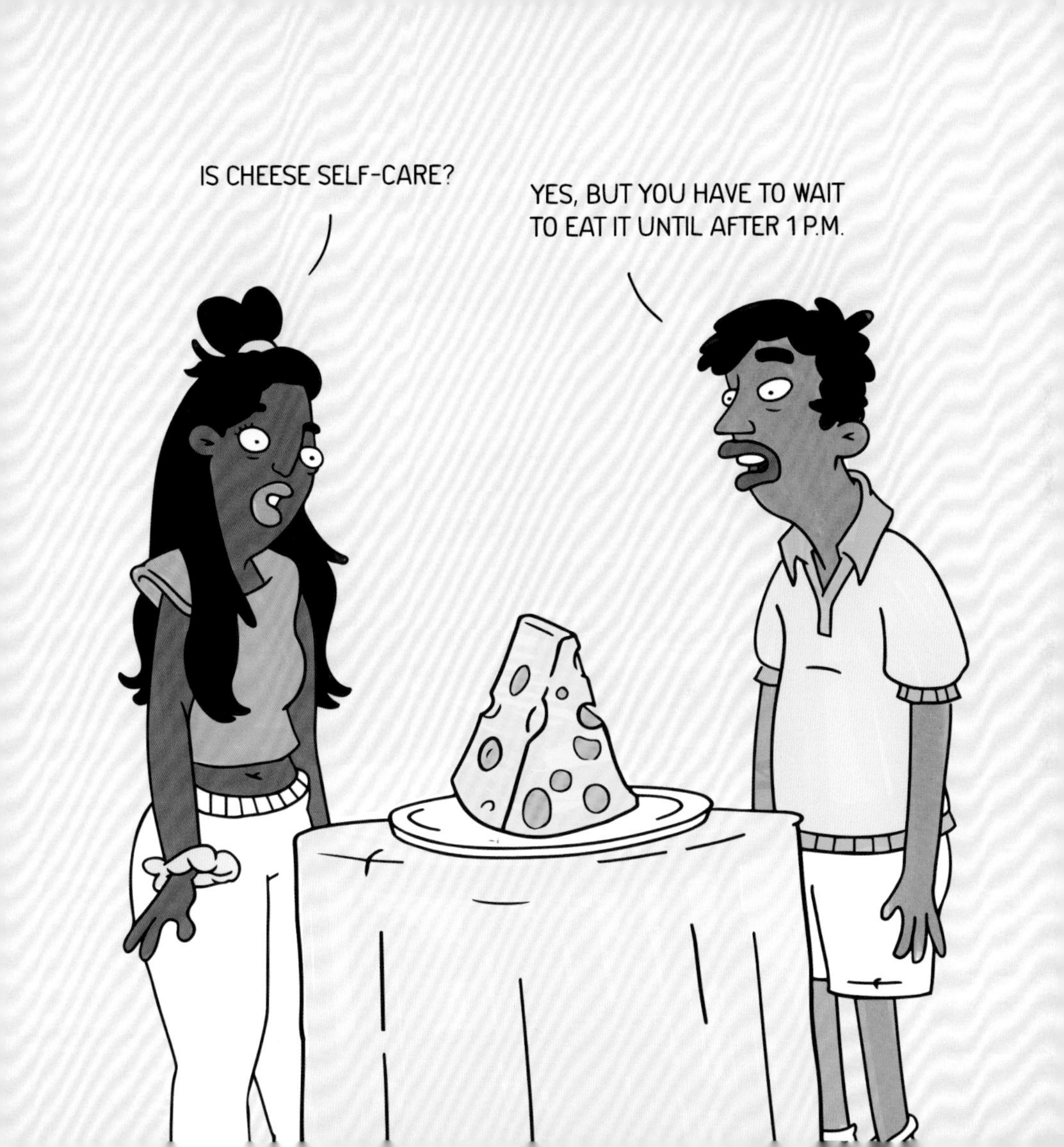
IS CHEESE SELF-CARE?
YES, BUT YOU HAVE TO WAIT TO EAT IT UNTIL AFTER 1 P.M.

You can't even keep your houseplants alive, and yet you're still expected to know how to manage your own microbiome.

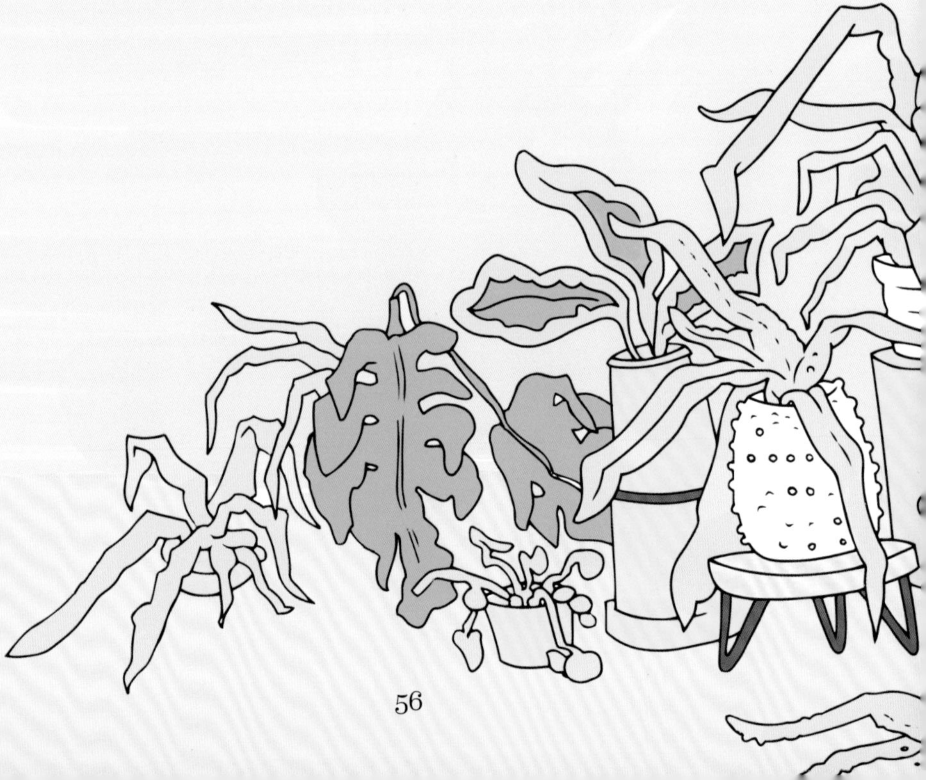

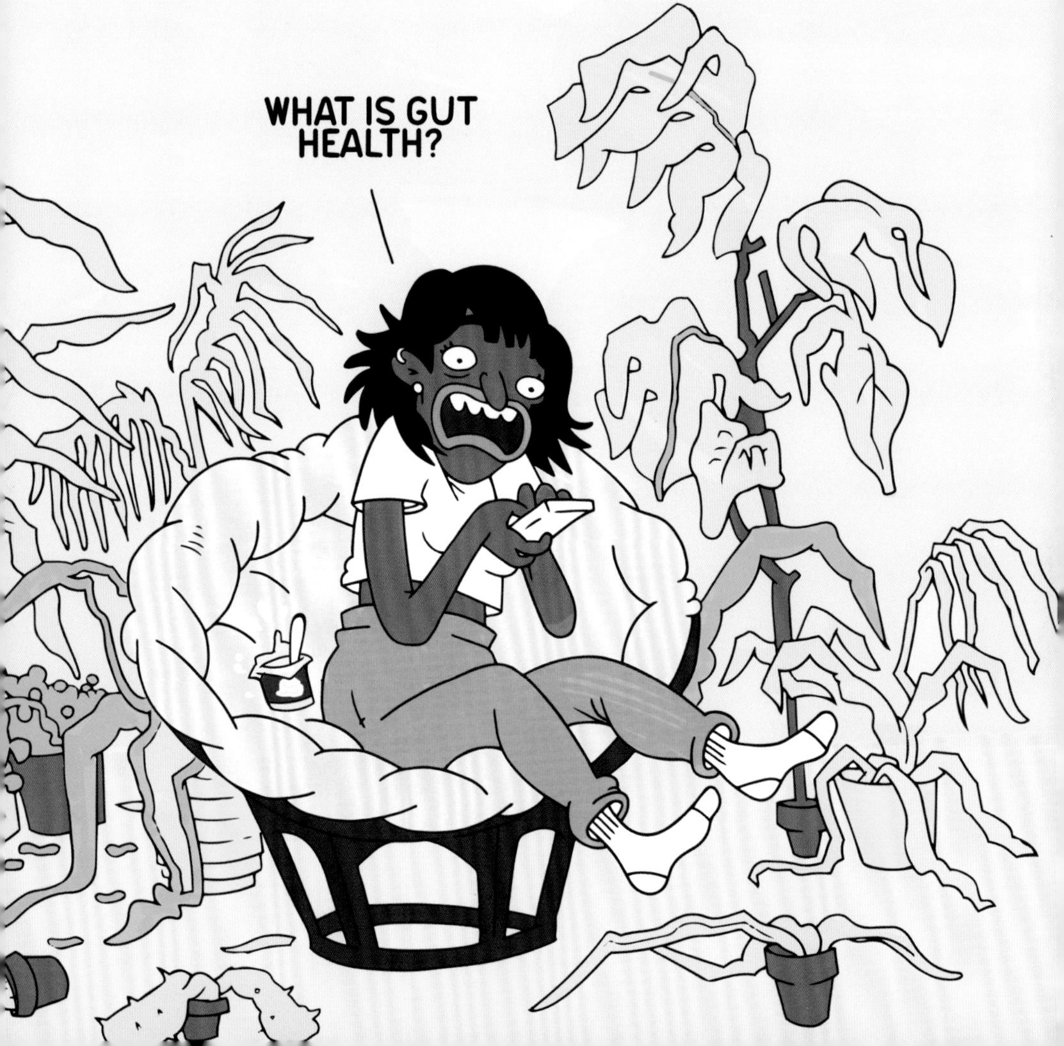
WHAT IS GUT HEALTH?

Self-diagnosing has
never been easier, though.

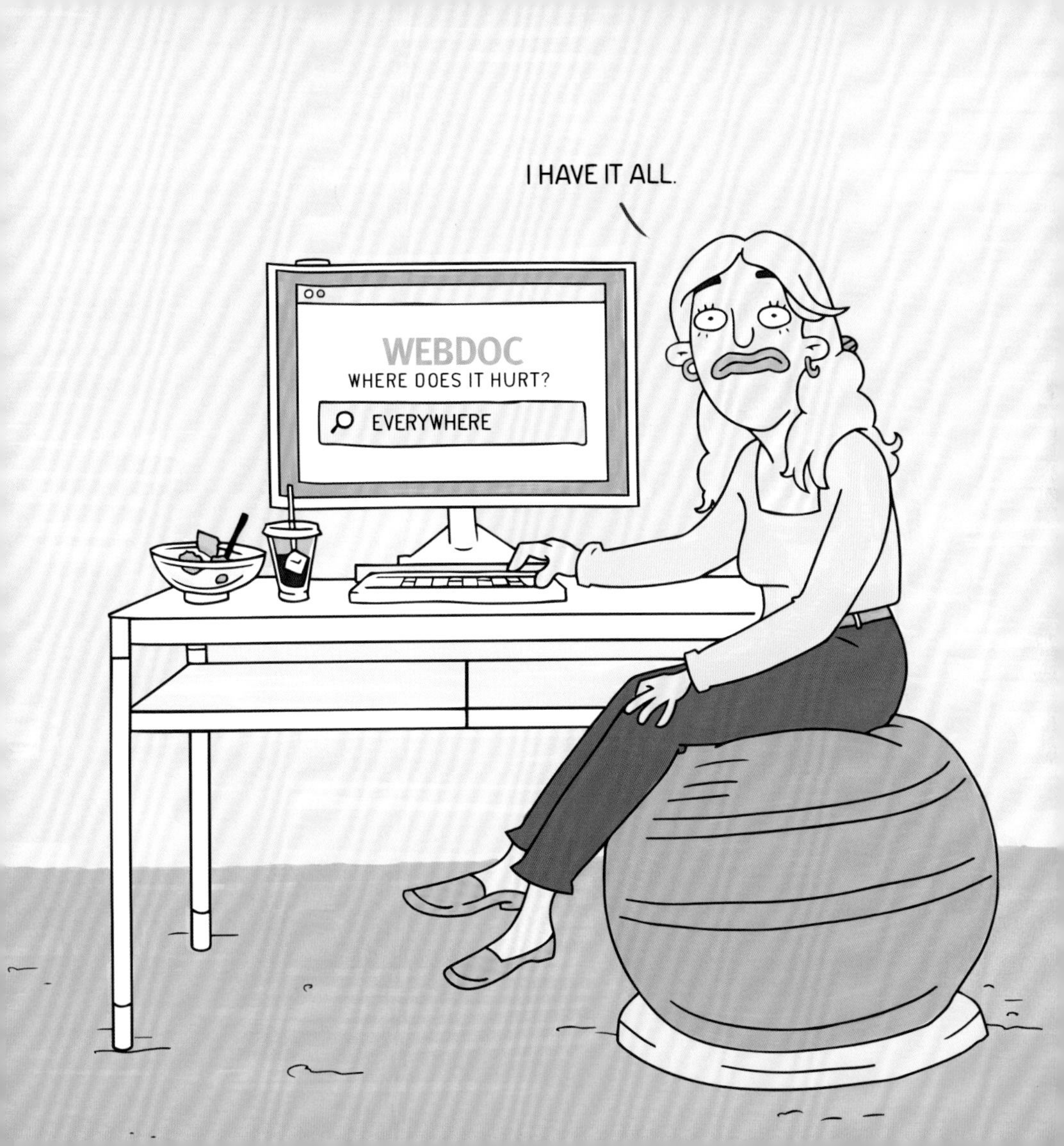

WEBDOC
WHERE DOES IT HURT?
EVERYWHERE
I HAVE IT ALL.

Lipstick. How are we supposed
to feel about lipstick right now?

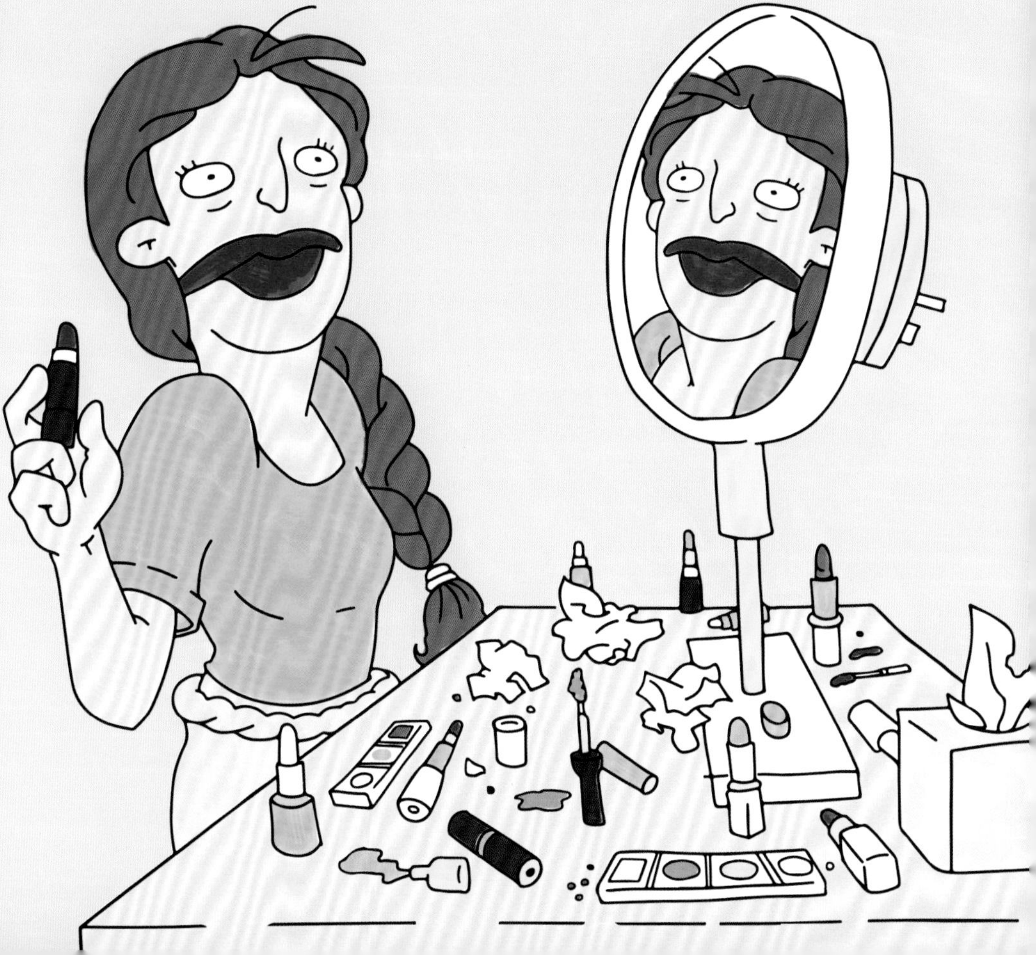

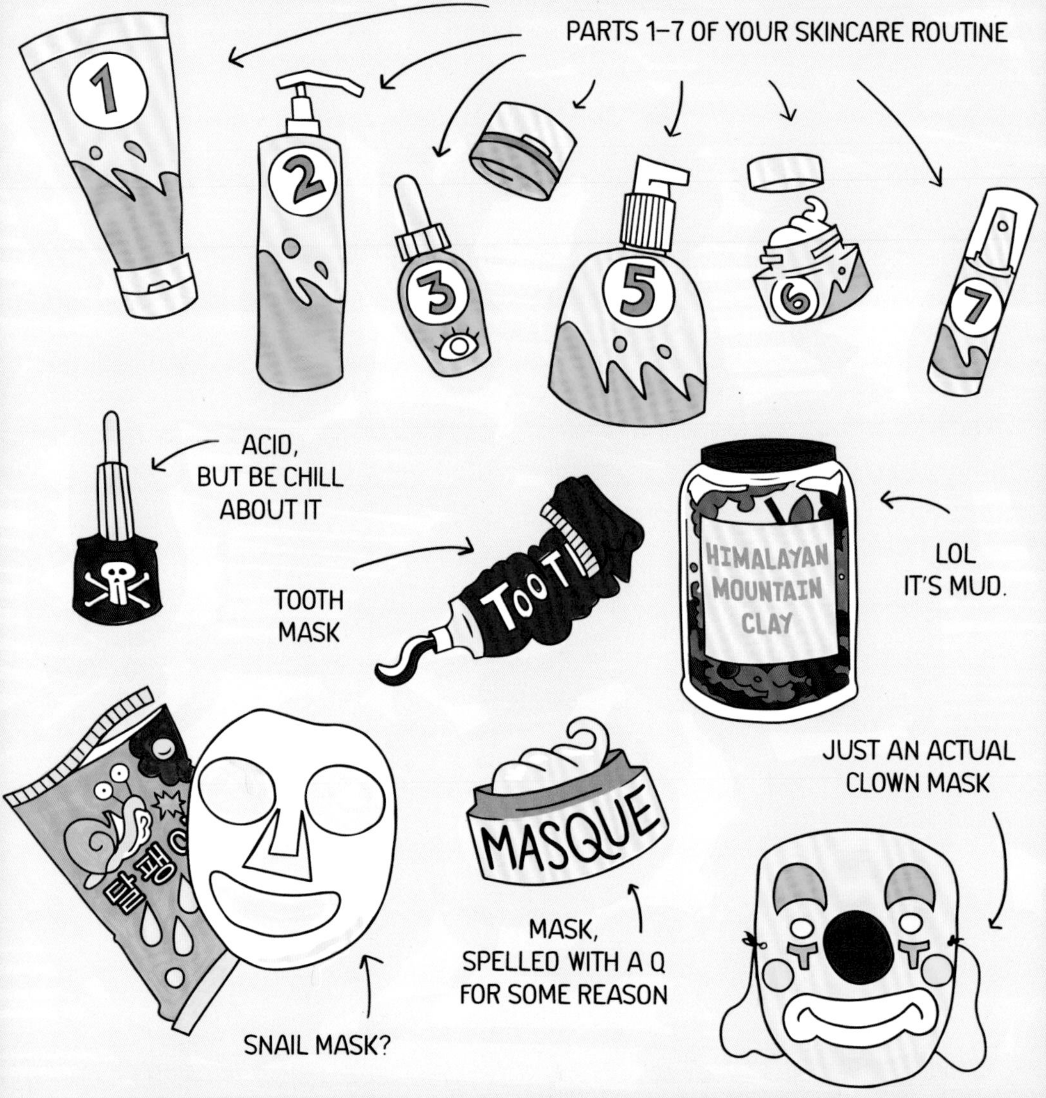
PARTS 1–7 OF YOUR SKINCARE ROUTINE
ACID,
BUT BE CHILL
ABOUT IT
TOOTH
MASK
TOOT
HIMALAYAN
MOUNTAIN
CLAY
LOL
IT'S MUD.
JUST AN ACTUAL
CLOWN MASK
MASQUE
MASK,
SPELLED WITH A Q
FOR SOME REASON
SNAIL MASK?

Every face cream you get
is part of a "system."

I JUST WANT TO BE
BEAUTIFUL!

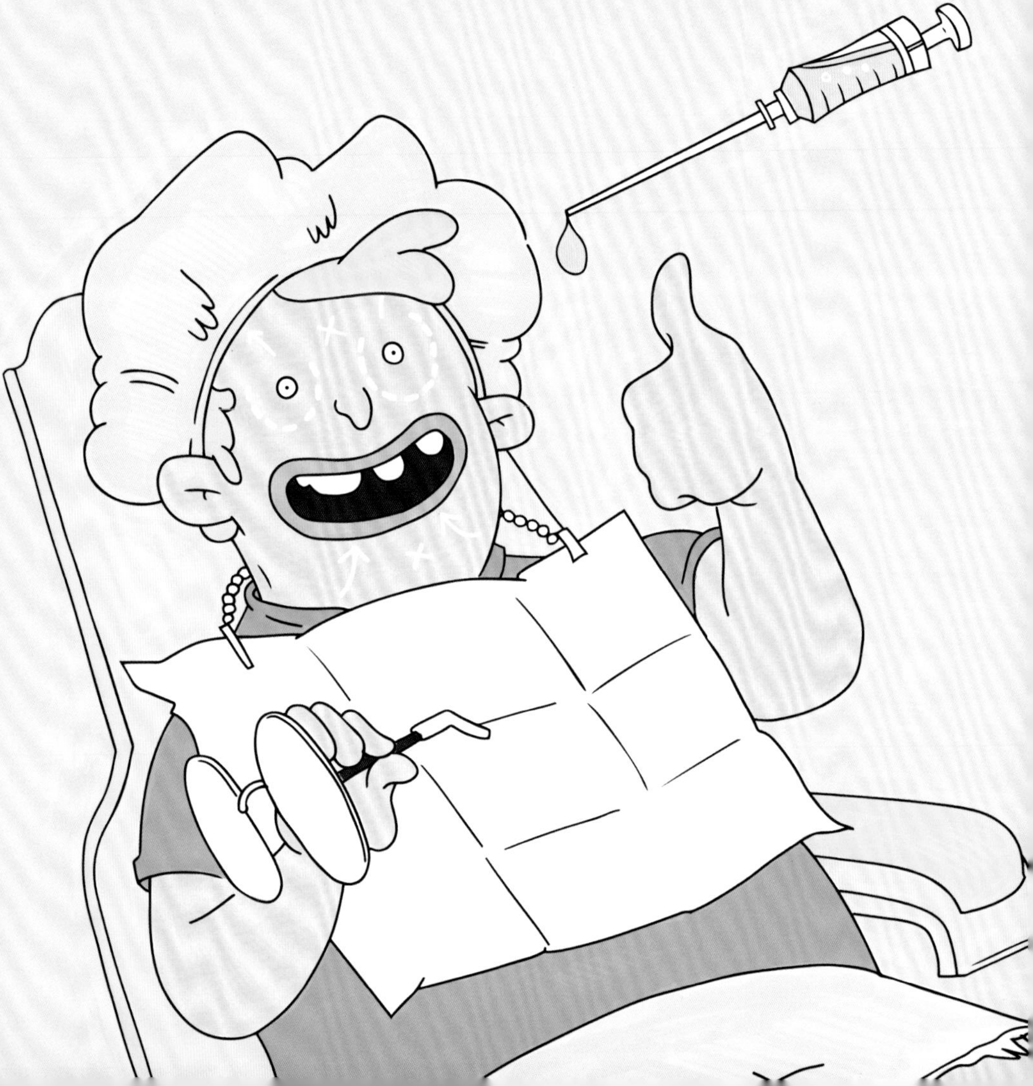

Don't worry, you'll still need Botox.

You can have a job,
or you can return your online purchases.

You can't have both.

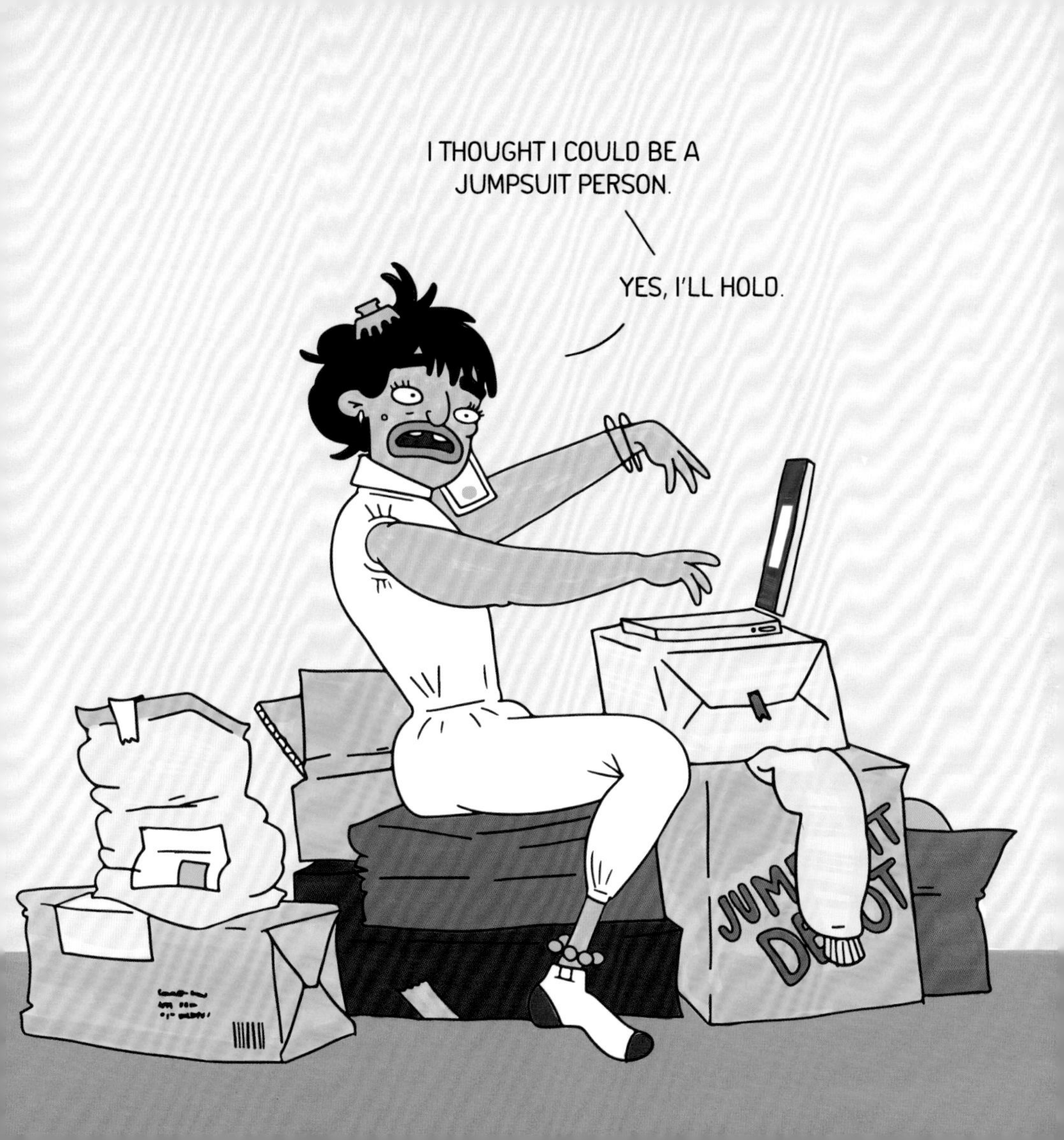
I THOUGHT I COULD BE A JUMPSUIT PERSON.
YES, I'LL HOLD.

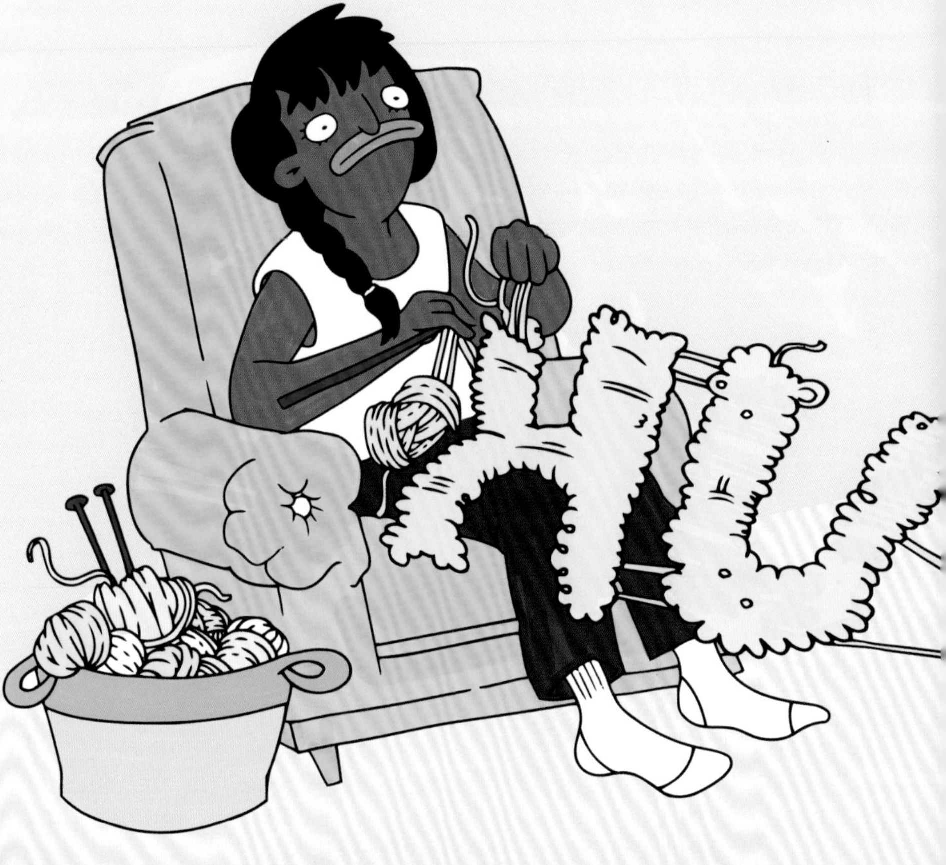

Hobbies are dead.

Now everything is just an alternative
revenue stream you haven't monetized yet.

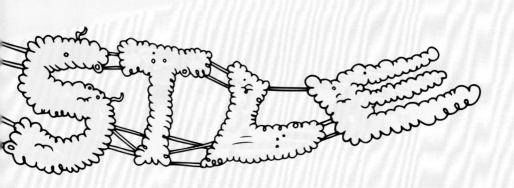

USB drives are changing at the speed of light.

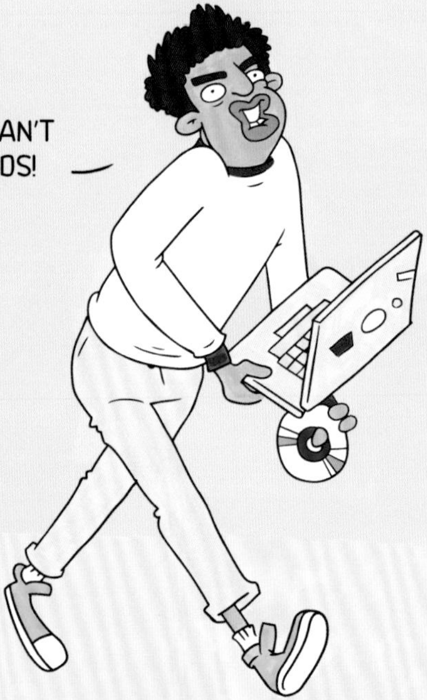
AND I STILL CAN'T PLAY MY DVDS!

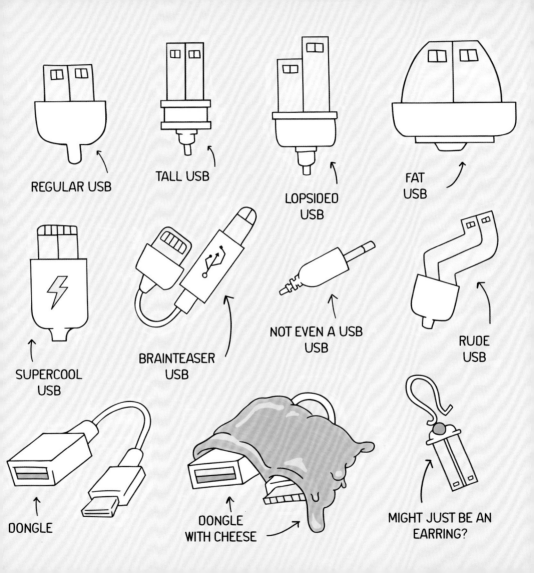

REGULAR USB

TALL USB

LOPSIDED USB

FAT USB

SUPERCOOL USB

BRAINTEASER USB

NOT EVEN A USB USB

RUDE USB

DONGLE

DONGLE WITH CHEESE

MIGHT JUST BE AN EARRING?

Your algorithms shape your personality, which in turn shapes your algorithms.

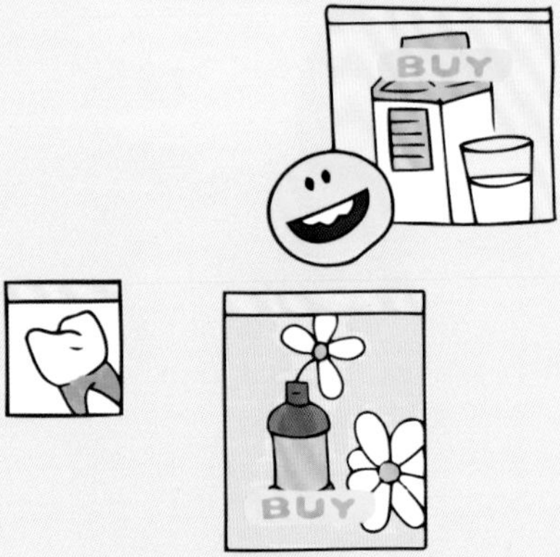
BUY
BUY

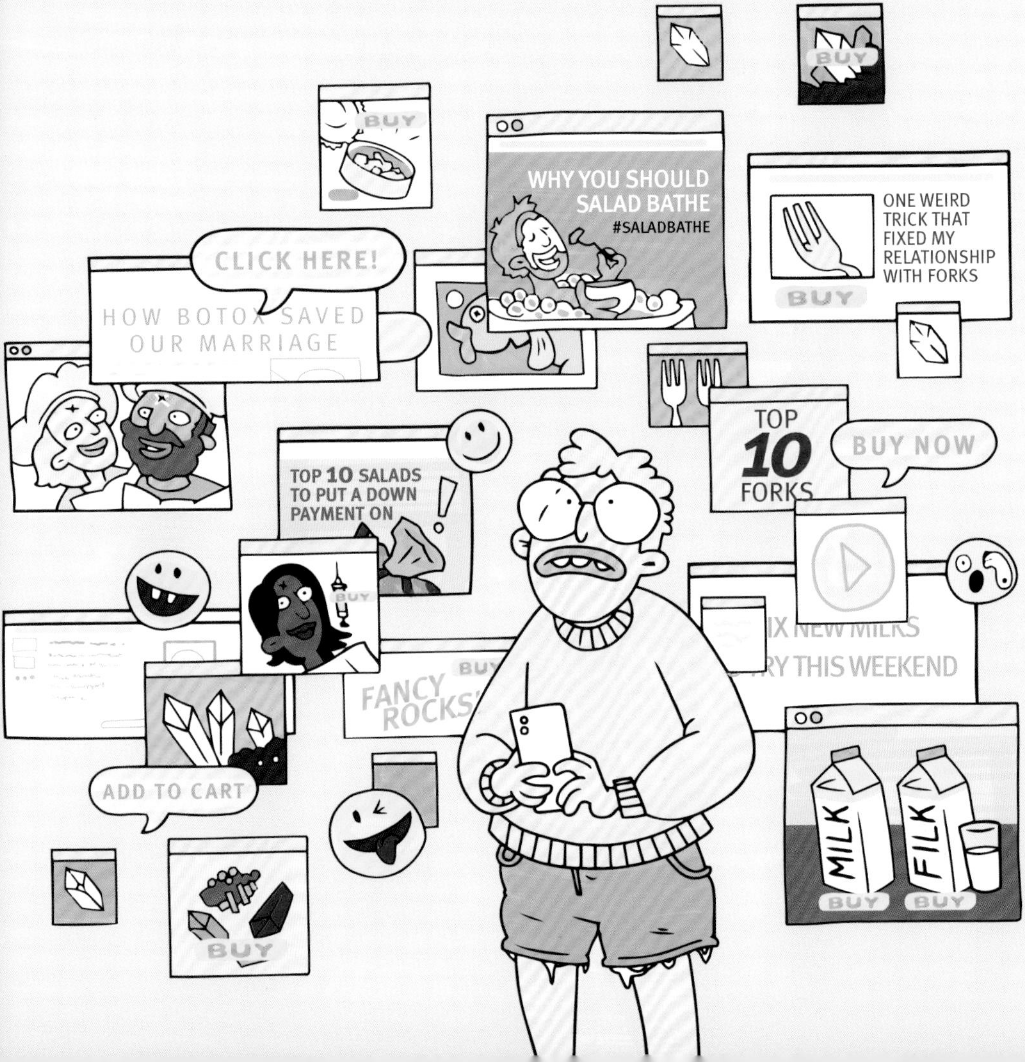
BUY
WHY YOU SHOULD SALAD BATHE
#SALADBATHE
ONE WEIRD TRICK THAT FIXED MY RELATIONSHIP WITH FORKS
BUY
CLICK HERE!
HOW BOTOX SAVED OUR MARRIAGE
TOP 10 FORKS
BUY NOW
TOP 10 SALADS TO PUT A DOWN PAYMENT ON
BUY
FANCY ROCKS!
IX NEW MILKS
RY THIS WEEKEND
ADD TO CART
MILK
FILK
BUY
BUY
BUY

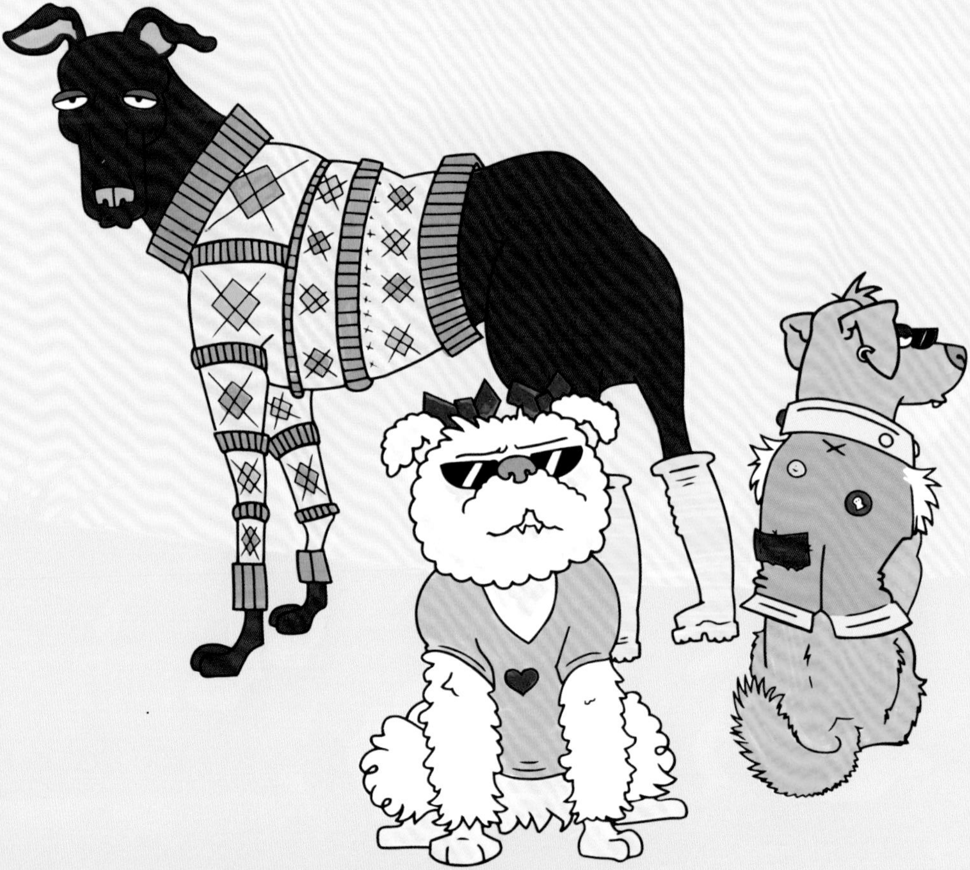

On the upside, dogs have never dressed better!

75

On the downside, sometimes they're dressed better than you.

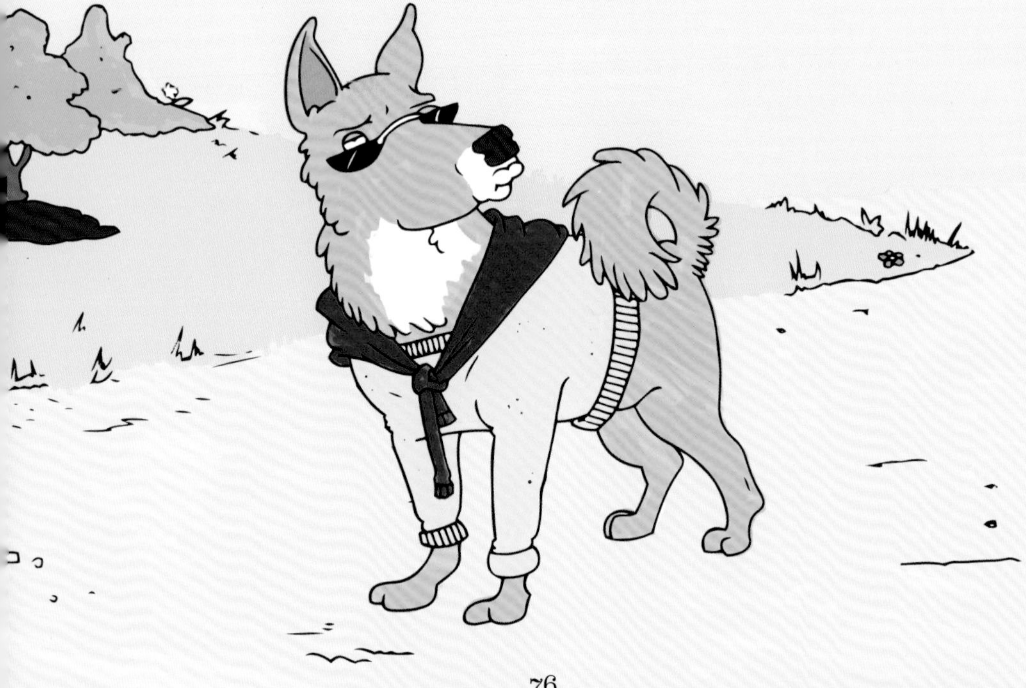

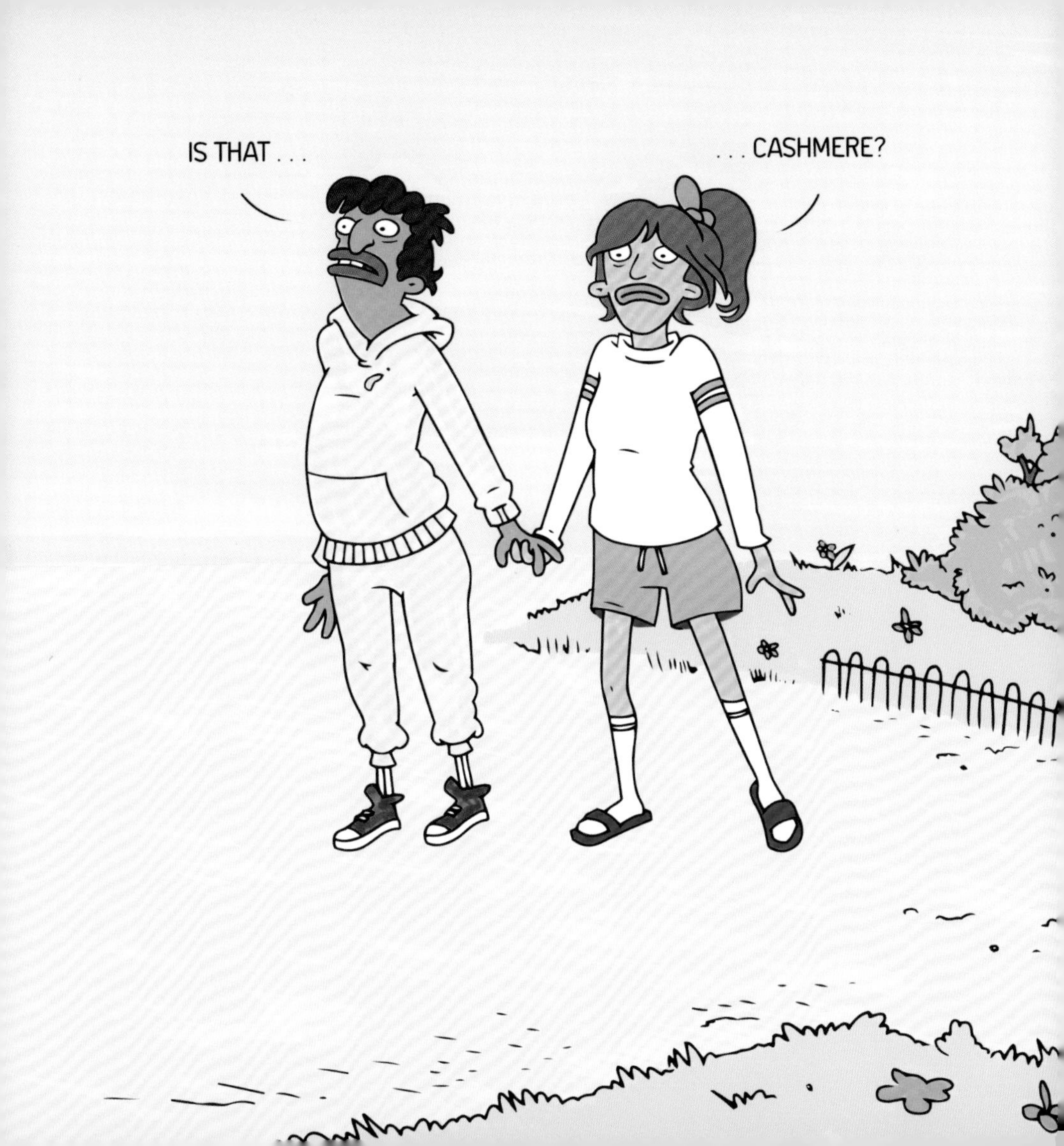
IS THAT . . .
. . . CASHMERE?

You'll always be acutely aware of the things you weren't invited to.

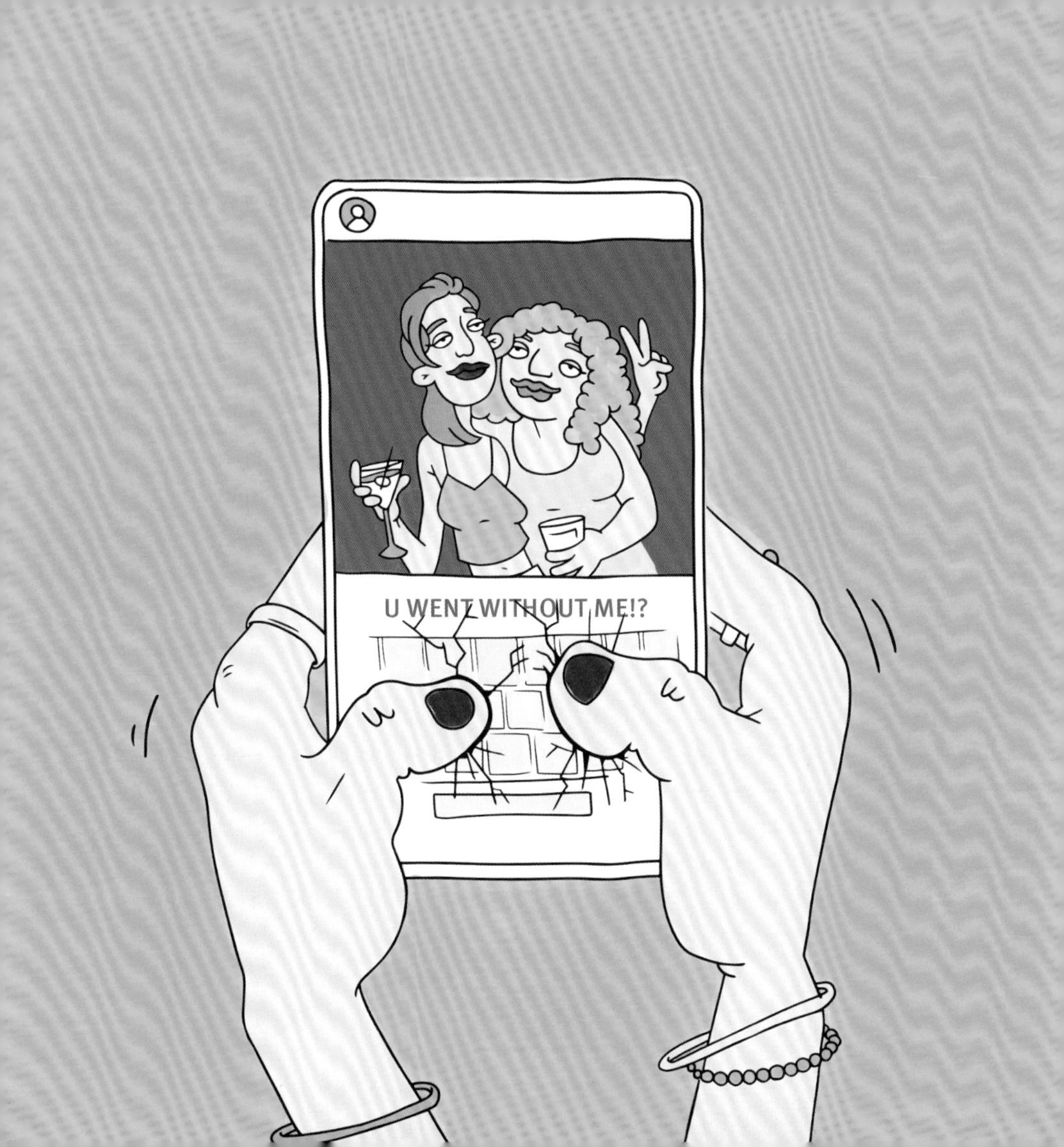
U WENT WITHOUT ME!?

You can only find out you're too old to "go hard" the hard way.

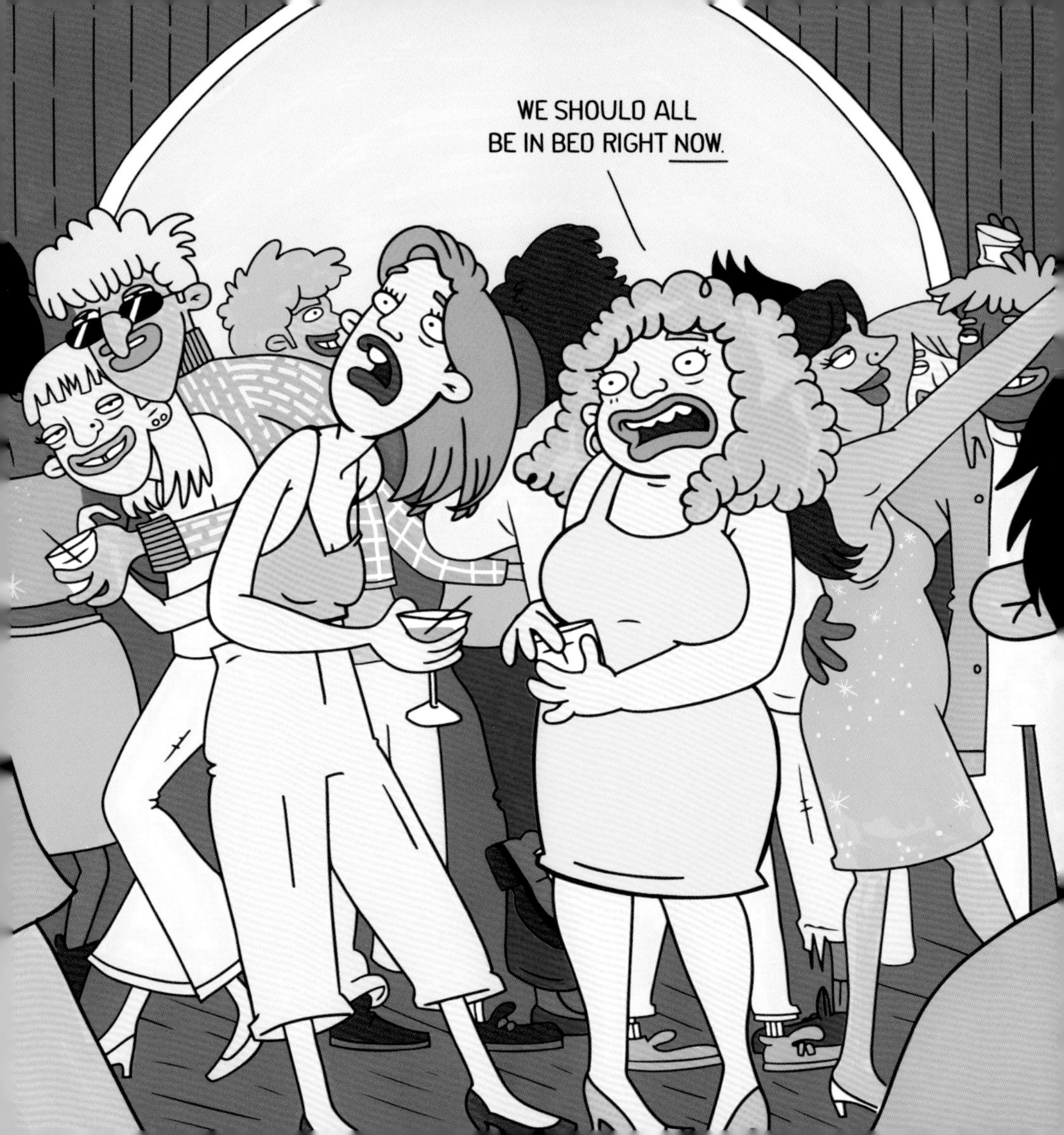
WE SHOULD ALL
BE IN BED RIGHT NOW.

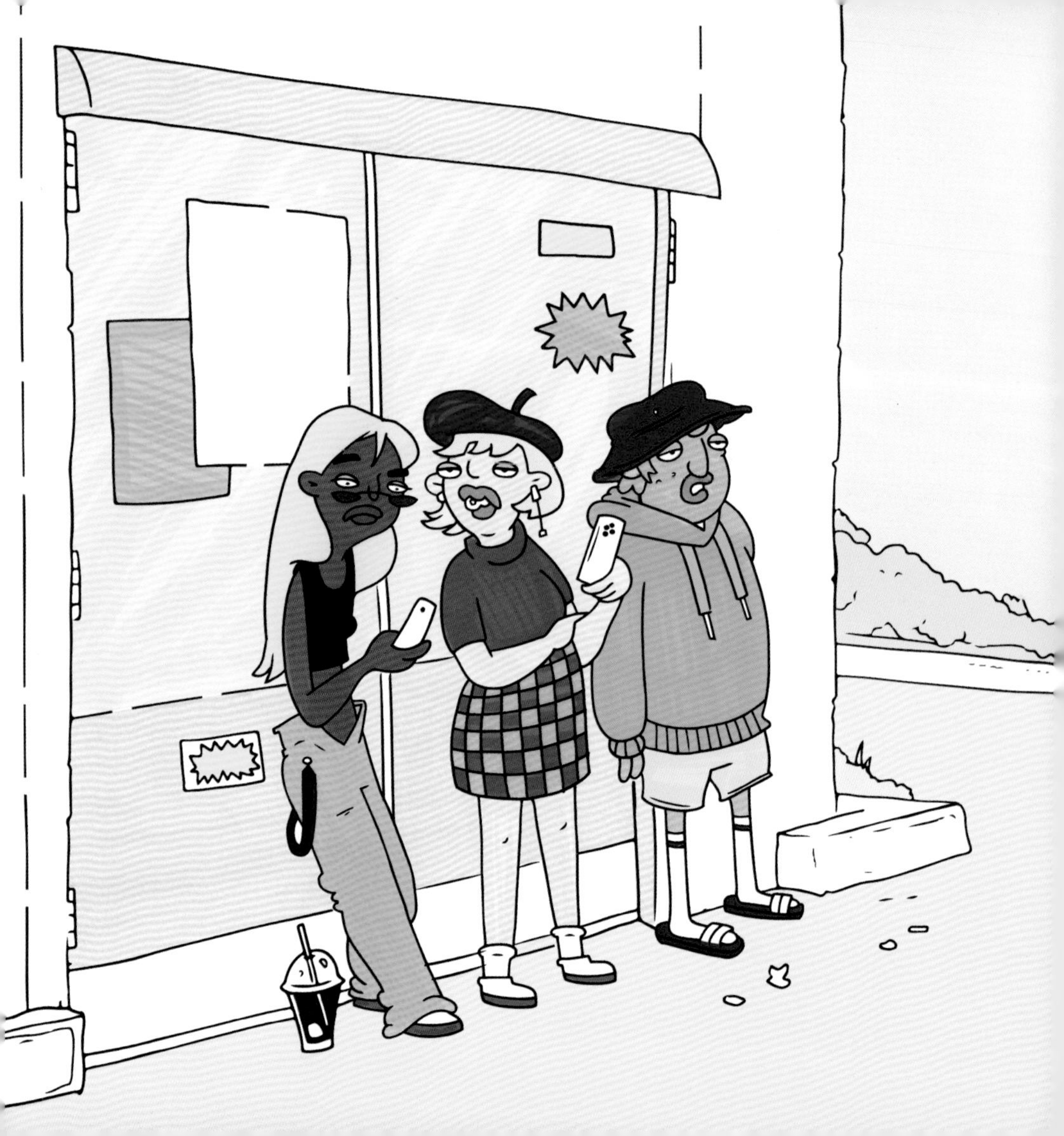

Teens have never been more intimidating.

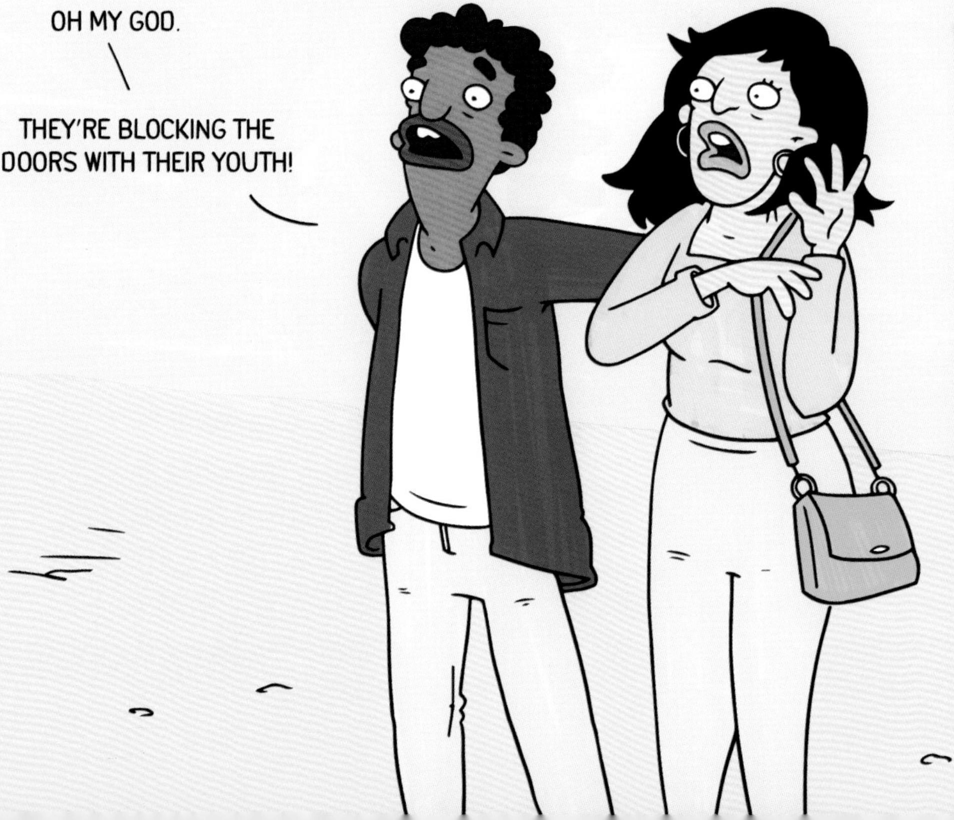
OH MY GOD.
THEY'RE BLOCKING THE DOORS WITH THEIR YOUTH!

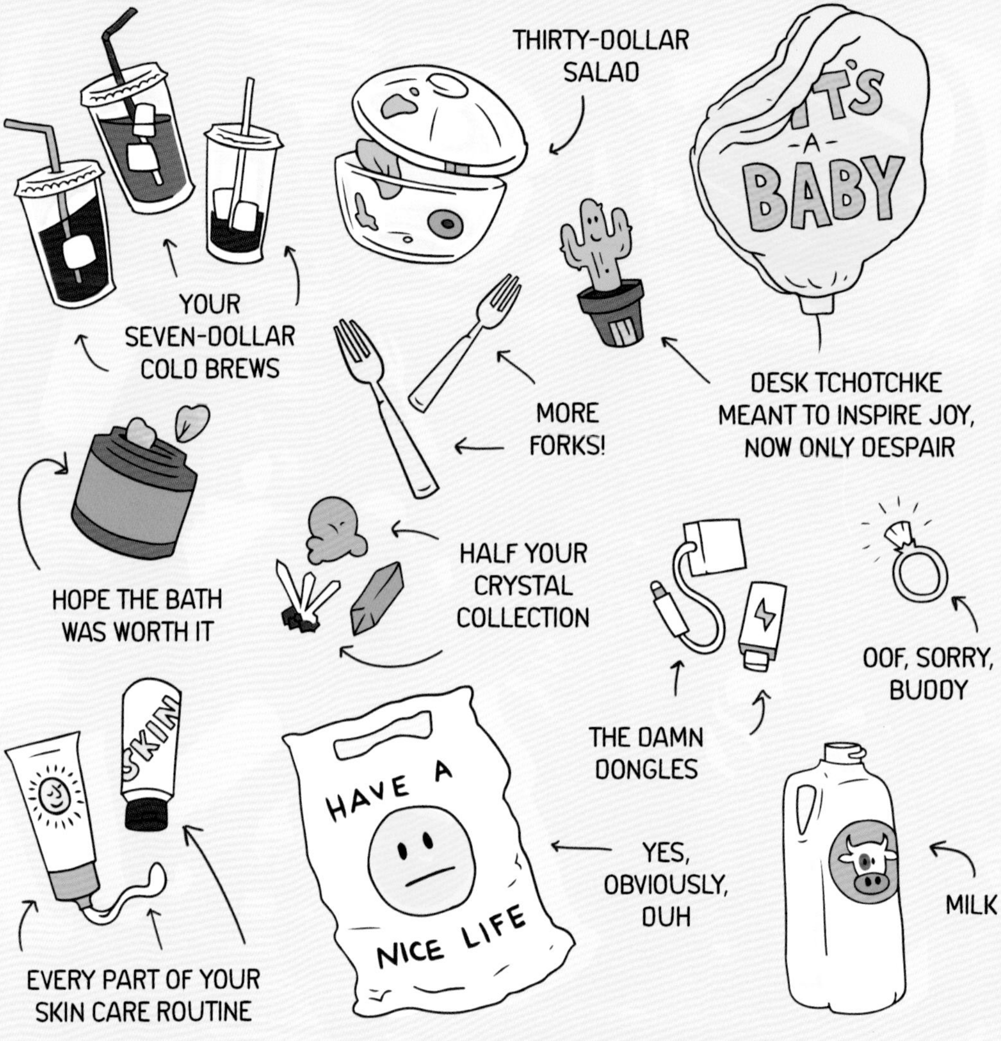
THIRTY-DOLLAR SALAD
IT'S A BABY
YOUR SEVEN-DOLLAR COLD BREWS
MORE FORKS!
DESK TCHOTCHKE MEANT TO INSPIRE JOY, NOW ONLY DESPAIR
HOPE THE BATH WAS WORTH IT
HALF YOUR CRYSTAL COLLECTION
OOF, SORRY, BUDDY
THE DAMN DONGLES
SKIN
HAVE A NICE LIFE
YES, OBVIOUSLY, DUH
MILK
EVERY PART OF YOUR SKIN CARE ROUTINE

Buying anything that has plastic is very bad, and everything is plastic.

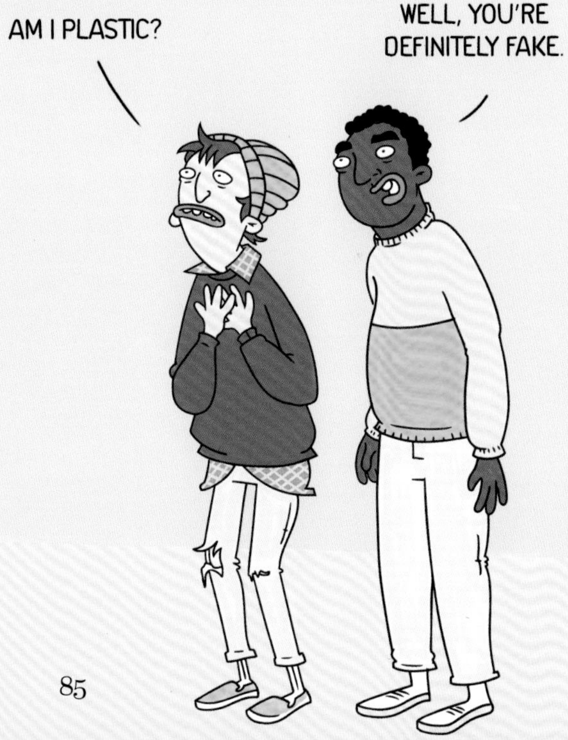
AM I PLASTIC?
WELL, YOU'RE DEFINITELY FAKE.

Oh shit, were we supposed to be composting this whole time?

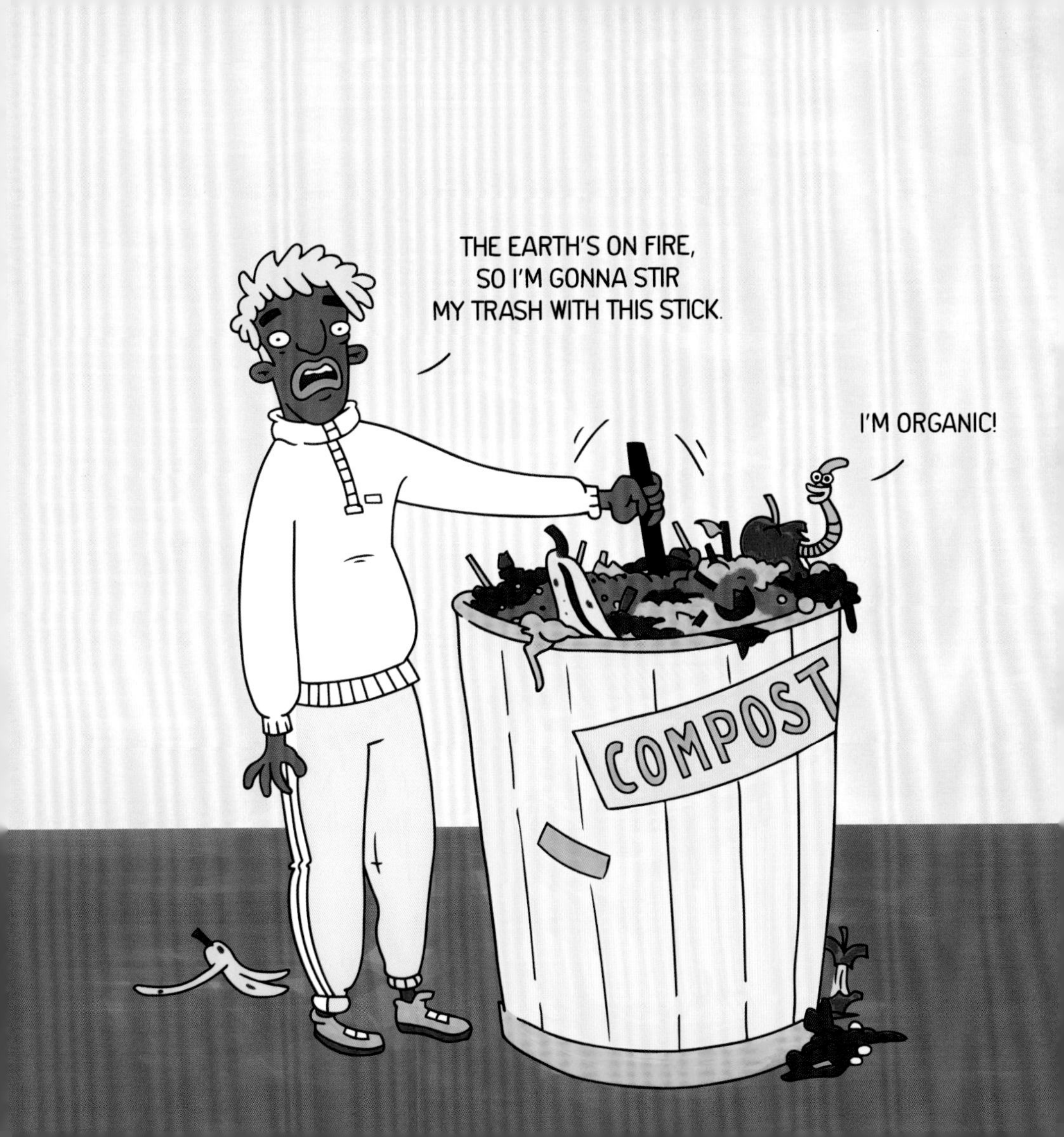
THE EARTH'S ON FIRE, SO I'M GONNA STIR MY TRASH WITH THIS STICK.
I'M ORGANIC!
COMPOST

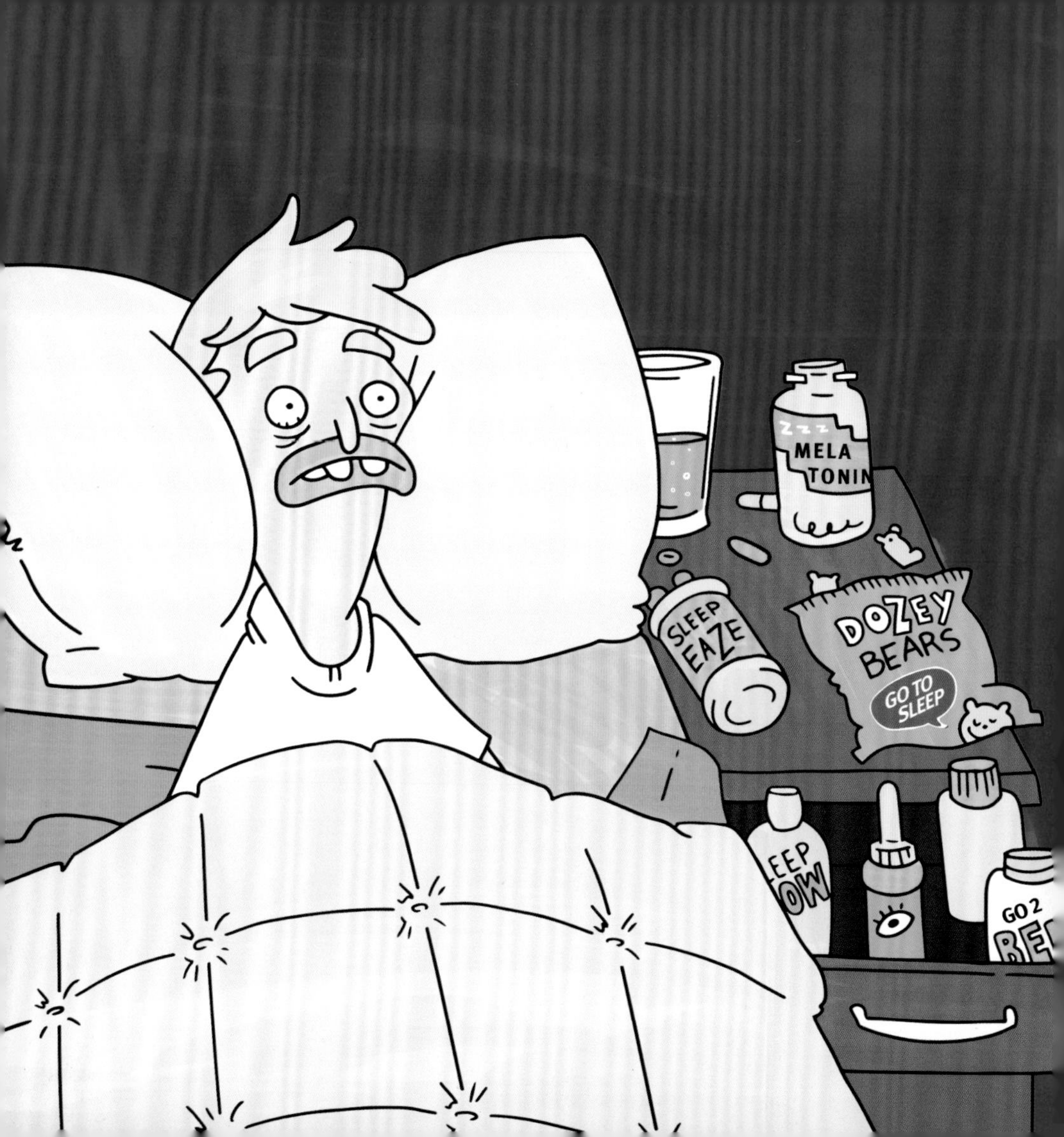
MELA
TONIN
SLEEP
EAZE
DOZEY
BEARS
GO TO
SLEEP
GO2

It's a lot.

Good news, though.

Humans are living longer than ever.

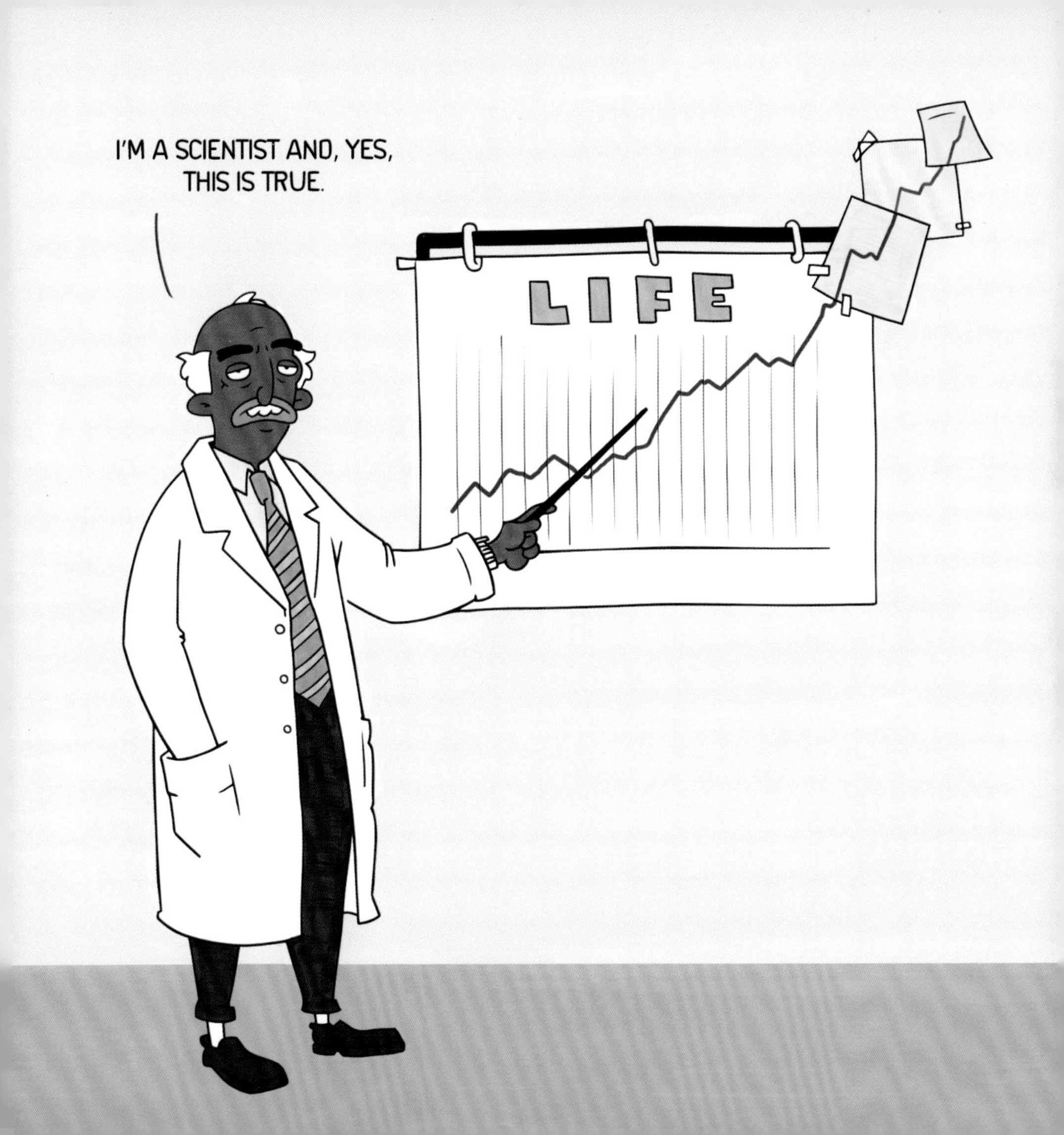
I'M A SCIENTIST AND, YES, THIS IS TRUE.
LIFE

So you can do this for longer!

THERE ARE SIX BILLION
NEW PLATFORMS I CAN TRY.

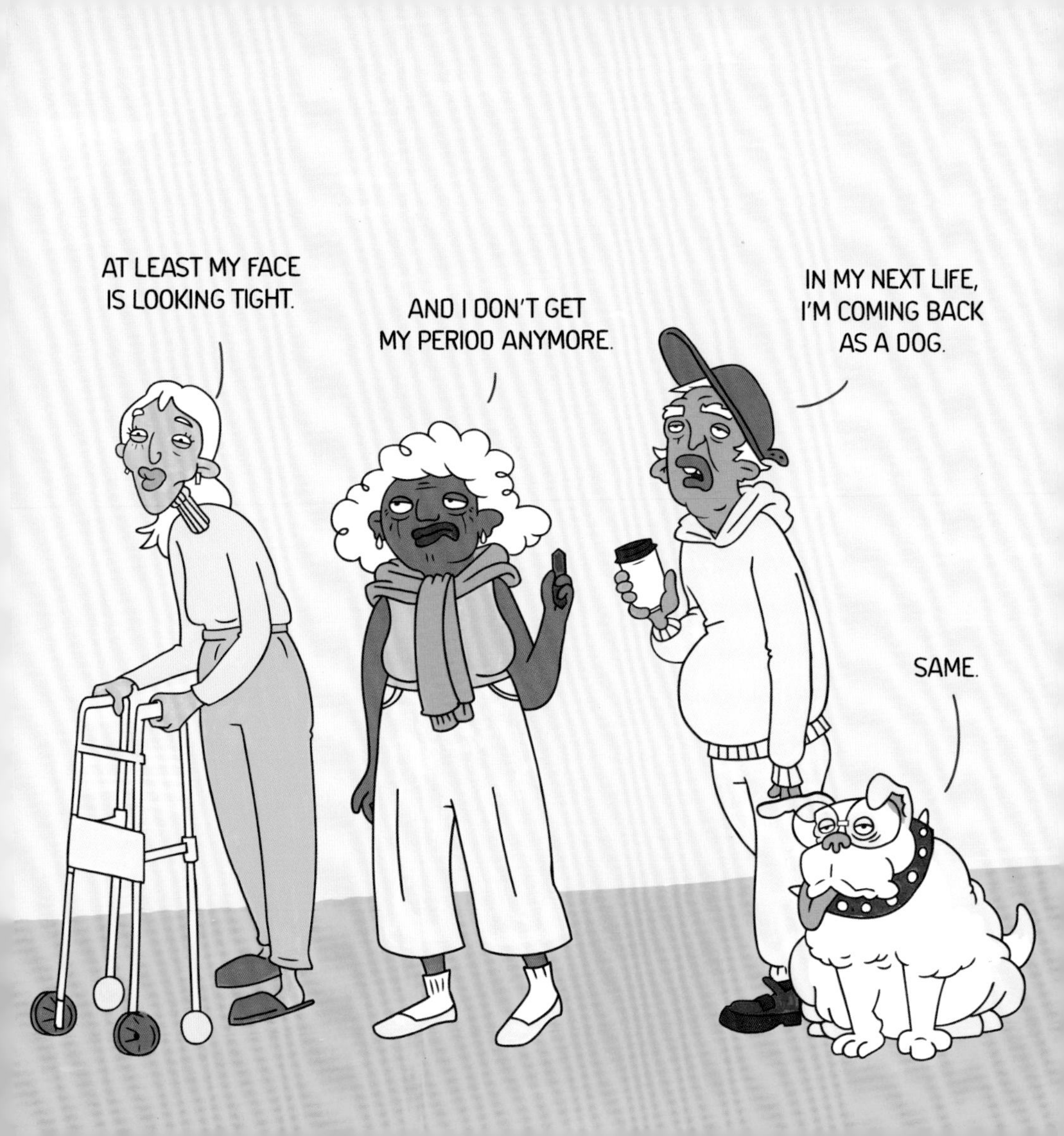
AT LEAST MY FACE IS LOOKING TIGHT.
AND I DON'T GET MY PERIOD ANYMORE.
IN MY NEXT LIFE, I'M COMING BACK AS A DOG.
SAME.

Big thanks to the book people at Chronicle, especially Olivia Roberts, Jon Glick, and Becca Hunt, and our lovely book agent, Joseph Perry. We never thought the art of complaining could become our art, but here we are.

Also big thanks to the people who created us and tolerate us on a daily basis, including Jeremy, Cora, and Rhett Straight; Ken and JoAnn Lawall; Tracy, Adam, Nate, and Tyler/Jason Coffman; Jessica, Jack, Kate, and Reagan Callender; Sara Shelton; Rich Greco; Dan Brill; Ed, Elizabeth, Tom, Colleen, and Carly Wonder; Julien Bauer; Emily Hovis; Anne Dellinger; Madeleine Trebenski; and the CEO of Oatly.

And to anyone else who has been in a group chat with either of us in the last three years. You know who you are, and we are sorry and you're welcome.

Tara Lawall is a writer, mother of two, and wife to one, who will use the proceeds of this book to fund more Botox. She complains for free on Twitter @TaraLawall and Instagram @TaraLawall.

Anne Marie Wonder is a writer and illustrator who spends her free time being aggrieved by almost everything. She is on Instagram @dirtydinorock.

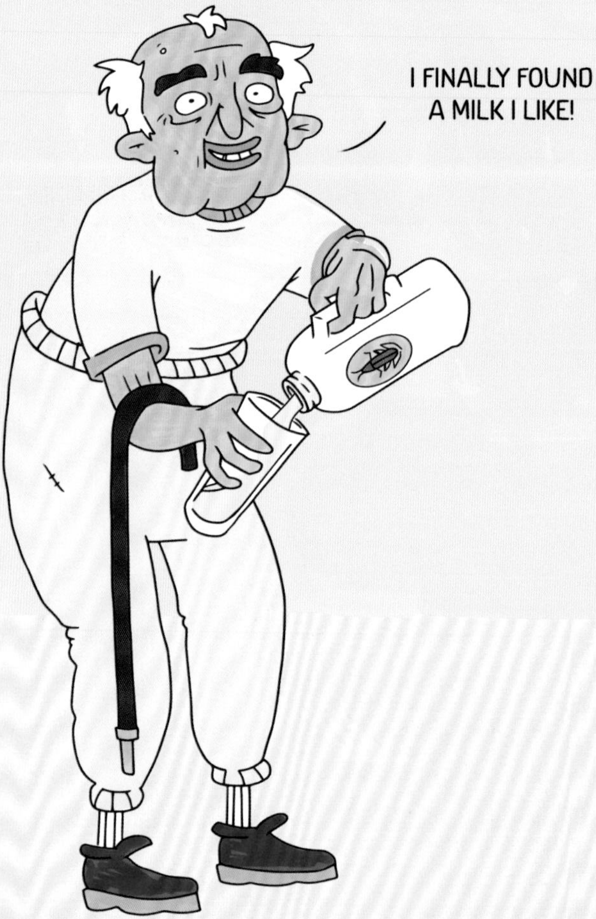
I FINALLY FOUND
A MILK I LIKE!